THE

Cricket
Quiz Book

by Chris Bradshaw

First published in 2008 by Collins
An imprint of HarperCollins*Publishers*
77–85 Fulham Palace Road
Hammersmith, London
W6 8JB

www.collins.co.uk

Reprint 10 9 8 7 6 5 4 3 2 1

The Times is a registered trademark of Times Newspapers Ltd

ISBN 978-0-00-727081-1

A catalogue record for this book is available from the British Library

Printed and bound in Great Britain by Clays Ltd, St Ives plc.

Mixed Sources
Product group from well-managed
forests and other controlled sources
www.fsc.org   Cert no. SW-COC-1806
© 1996 Forest Stewardship Council

FSC is a non-profit international organisation established to promote the
responsible management of the world's forests. Products carrying the FSC
label are independently certified to assure consumers that they come
from forests that are managed to meet the social, economic and
ecological needs of present and future generations.

Foreword

I have been writing and talking about cricket for longer than I care to think (exactly *how* long is, happily, not one of the questions that follow) but I have to confess that I am hopeless at quizzes myself. If, for example, I know the answer in the general knowledge section of *Mastermind*, I am always beaten to the draw by the contestant; and when I see questions on paper that I ought to be able to answer with ease, my mind freezes as it used to when confronted by one of those school mathematics problems ... If a man drives to Leicester at 48 miles per hour and Leicester is 24 miles distant, how long will it take him to arrive? Ugh. I can feel the blush on my cheeks still, even as pupils all around me put up their hands and said, 'Sir, sir ... oh, Sirrrr ...'

But this book is different. Most of the questions are not too difficult, which is good, because people like to know the answers to some questions at least: it is good for their peace of mind. Many of the questions are admirably topical, which is not always the case with quizzes. There are enough sufficiently tricky ones to sort the serious scholars from the amateurs. There are a few multiple choice questions too, which always makes life easier. And they are all about cricket, not maths, or French, or the reason for the Great Atlantic Drift; or the formula for hydrogen; or the date of the battle of Agincourt. (I know that everyone knows that Agincourt was in 1415, but that's not the point.)

Above all, this is the most wide-ranging cricket quiz book I have seen. It covers everything from the early days of international cricket to recent Twenty20 contests.

I have been able to give the questions only an overview so far, but I shall keep it by my bed in future. It will induce a satisfied sleep much more certainly than a crossword or one of those infuriating Su Doku puzzles.

Quiz books are, indeed, like anthologies, or favourite old films: they need to be looked at and enjoyed from time to time, when the mood is right and the brain is in tune; not dealt with in a single session like an exam. You can take as much or as little time as you wish over these gentle tests of your knowledge. And if you, too, put it on your bedside table, try to resist looking up the answer to something that is on the edge of your brain – at least until the morning. It may come to you at three in the morning and your sleep will be blissful after that.

Christopher Martin-Jenkins

Introduction

Which pair of brothers made their One Day International debut in the same match but for different countries? Which West Indian wicketkeeper went on to become a diplomat at the United Nations? Who holds the record for the most Test match ducks in a career? Find out the answers to these and many more cricket testers in *The Times Cricket Quiz Book*.

Whether it's the leisurely pace of the county game, the crash, bang, wallop of Twenty20 or the subtle fluctuations of a Test match that appeal, we've got questions for you. Test yourself on the great batsmen, bowlers and fielders, captains and record breakers, the politics and literature, not forgetting the all important Laws of the game. We also look at some of the more obscure aspects of cricket from great beards and moustaches to the remarkable number of Grahams in the game. It's not just England either. We've covered the whole of the cricketing world from Australia to Pakistan, Sri Lanka to the West Indies and just about everywhere in between. With seven unique categories featuring one hundred themed quizzes there's something for everyone from the novice cricket watcher to the seasoned observer.

So, whether it's fearsome fast bowlers, looping leg spinners or brutal big hitters you want to know about then jump on in. As the men in the white coat say.

Play.

Contents

Competitions

1 The Ashes
2 The Ashes 1981
3 The Ashes 2005
4 1975 World Cup.
5 1979 World Cup
6 1983 World Cup
7 1987 World Cup
8 1992 World Cup
9 1996 World Cup
10 1999 World Cup
11 2003 World Cup
12 2007 World Cup
13 World Twenty20 2007
14 English Domestic Competitions
15 English Twenty20 Cup
16 India versus Australia 2001
17 Sheffield Shield
18 World Series Cricket

The Greats

19 Ambrose and Walsh
20 Allan Border
21 Sir Ian Botham
22 Geoffrey Boycott
23 Sir Donald Bradman
24 Andrew Flintoff
25 Brian Lara

26 Lillee and Thomson
27 Muttiah Muralitharan
28 Kevin Pietersen
29 Sir Viv Richards
30 Sir Garfield Sobers
31 Sachin Tendulkar
32 Michael Vaughan
33 Shane Warne
34 Wasim and Waqar

Countries

35 Australia
36 Bangladesh
37 England
38 India
39 New Zealand
40 Pakistan
41 South Africa
42 Sri Lanka
43 West Indies
44 Zimbabwe

Counties

45 Derbyshire CCC
46 Durham CCC
47 Essex CCC
48 Glamorgan CCC
49 Gloucestershire CCC
50 Hampshire CCC
51 Kent CCC

52 Lancashire CCC

53 Leicestershire CCC

54 Middlesex CCC

55 Northamptonshire CCC

56 Nottinghamshire CCC

57 Somerset CCC

58 Surrey CCC

59 Sussex CCC

60 Warwickshire CCC

61 Worcestershire CCC

62 Yorkshire CCC

Out of the Ordinary

63 Anagrams

64 Bad Boys

65 Beards and Moustaches

66 Debuts

67 Family Affairs

68 Golden Grahams

69 Injuries

70 Name Game

71 One Test Wonders

72 Portly Players

73 Quotes

Players

74 All Rounders

75 Big Hitters

76 Captains

77 In the Field

78 Left Arm Seamers

79 Left Arm Spinners

80 Left-Handed Batsmen

81 Off Spinners

82 Opening Batsmen

83 Record Breakers: Test Matches

84 Record Breakers: One Day Internationals

85 Smell the Leather: Pacemen

86 Swingers and Seamers

87 Tailenders

88 West Indian Bowlers

89 Wicket-keepers

90 Wrist Spinners

Mixed Bag

91 Books

92 Grounds

93 Language of Cricket

94 Laws of the Game

95 Politics

96 Television

97 Test Match Special

98 Trophies and Awards

99 Umpires

100 Women's Cricket

Answers

The Ashes

1 In what year was the first Test match between Australia and England played: 1867, 1877 or 1887?

2 What was the score in the 2006/07 Ashes series?

3 Which English batsman scored hundreds in three consecutive Tests in the 1986/87 series?

4 Who captained England to victory in the 1970/71 Ashes series?

5 Which England batsman played 15 Ashes Test matches between 1989 and 1993 but was never on a winning side?

6 Who in the 2005 Ashes series became the first bowler to dismiss Matthew Hayden for a Test match golden duck?

7 Which Australian almost died after chewing gum became stuck in his throat after being hit by a Bob Willis delivery?

8 The Centenary Tests were held at which two grounds?

9 The 1977 Test at Headingley was disrupted after the pitch had been damaged by campaigners trying to free which alleged armed robber?

10 Who was the captain of the first Australian side to whitewash England in an Ashes series: Warwick Armstrong, Steve Waugh or Ricky Ponting?

Answers on page 208

11 Which Australian was over 50 years old when he played in the Bodyline series in 1932/33?

12 Who scored a then record innings of 364 in the 1938 Ashes series?

13 Which Australian debutant smashed Tony Greig for five consecutive boundaries in the first Centenary Test?

14 Which two future captains scored maiden Test centuries as Australia compiled a mammoth 601 for seven in the First Test at Headingley in 1989?

15 What is the highest innings in an Ashes Test match: 703, 803 or 903?

16 What was remarkable about the result of the Australian Centenary Test?

17 England beat Australia by three runs at the MCG in 1982. Who took the crucial last wicket?

18 How many times did Alec Stewart win the toss in the five match Ashes series in 1998/99?

19 Who scored an unbeaten 173 at Headingley to steer England to their one and only victory in the 2001 Ashes series?

20 Which ground will host its first Ashes Test in 2009?

Answers on page 208

QUIZ 2 The Ashes 1981

1 Who won the first Test match at Trent Bridge?

2 How many runs did Ian Botham score in the second Test at Lord's?

3 Who replaced Ian Botham as captain for the third Test at Headingley?

4 Who took six for 95 in Australia's first innings at Headingley?

5 What was England's first innings deficit in that game: 177, 197 or 227?

6 How many runs did Ian Botham score in the second innings at Headingley?

7 Botham put on 117 for the eighth wicket with which unlikely partner?

8 Complete Richie Benaud's famous line of commentary: 'Don't even bother looking for that one. It's gone straight into ...'

9 How many runs did Australia need to win at Headingley: 130, 140 or 150?

10 What were Bob Willis' bowling figures in the Australian second innings at Headingley?

11 Australia were set a target of 151 to win the fourth Test at Edgbaston. Who took five wickets for one run to steer England to victory?

12 How many runs did Ian Botham score in the second innings of the fifth Test at Old Trafford: 100, 118 or 149?

13 Which England tail ender made an unbeaten 52 on his Test debut at Old Trafford?

14 Who played his one and only Test match for England in the sixth Test at The Oval?

15 Which Australian, with 533 runs, was the leading run scorer in the 1981 Ashes series?

16 Who was the leading wicket taker in the series with 42 victims?

17 Three wicketkeepers played for England in the 1981 Ashes series. Who were they?

18 Who were the four Englishmen who played in all six Ashes Test matches in 1981?

19 Two players made two centuries in the series. Who were they?

20 True or false: Graham Dilley scored more runs in the series than Mike Brearley?

Answers on page 208

The Ashes 2005

1 What was the score in the Ashes 2005 series?

2 Who were the two captains?

3 Who won the first Test at Lord's?

4 Which England batsman made his debut in the first Test at Lord's: Ian Bell or Kevin Pietersen?

5 Which Australian bowler missed the Edgbaston Test after getting injured in the warm-up?

6 What was England's margin of victory in the 2nd Test at Edgbaston?

7 Which two England batsmen scored centuries in the third Test at Old Trafford?

8 Which Australian last wicket pair survived 24 balls at the end of day five to cling on for the draw?

9 Who took the last five wickets to fall in Australia's first innings at Old Trafford?

10 Who ran out Ricky Ponting in the fourth Test at Trent Bridge?

11 Ashley Giles hit the winning runs in the fourth Test. Who was batting at the other end?

12 Which Australian fast bowler made his Test debut in the Trent Bridge Test?

Answers on page 208

13 Who scored a century in England's first innings in the last Test at The Oval?

14 Australia lost their last seven wickets for how many runs in their 1st innings at The Oval: 44, 54 or 64?

15 Who scored 158 in England's second innings at The Oval?

16 Three England players scored over 400 runs in the 2005 Ashes series. Who were they?

17 How many wickets did Shane Warne take in the series: 30, 35 or 40?

18 How many players played for England throughout the series?

19 Shane Warne took his 600th and Glenn McGrath his 500th Test wicket during the series by dismissing which batsman?

20 Who was England's leading wicket taker in the series?

Answers on page 208

QUIZ 4   1975 Cricket World Cup

1   Which country hosted the first Cricket World Cup?

2   Who won the tournament?

3   Who were the runners-up?

4   How many teams took part in the tournament: 8, 10 or 12?

5   True or false: not a single game was interrupted by rain?

6   Who took 174 balls to make just 36 not out in a group game: Geoff Boycott, Sunil Gavaskar or Mike Brearley?

7   Which Englishman scored the first World Cup century?

8   Which New Zealander with 171 not out compiled the highest score in the tournament?

9   Which Indian spinner bowled a 12 over spell that conceded just 6 runs?

10   Javed Miandad made his One Day International debut in the competition. How old was he: 17, 18 or 19?

11   Deryck Murray added 64 for the last wicket with which bowler to claim an unlikely win over Pakistan: Michael Holding, Joel Garner or Andy Roberts?

12   Who ran out three batsmen in the final: Viv Richards, Ian Chappell or Clive Lloyd?

Answers on page 208

13 Which current English First Class Umpire played in the 1975 World Cup final?

14 Which Australian took six for 14 in the semi-final against England?

15 True or false: the highest individual score in the semi-final between England and Australia was just 28?

16 Which left-handed batsman scored 102 in the final?

17 True or false: all the West Indian players who appeared in the 1975 World Cup had previously played county cricket?

18 Which three West Indian greats made their One Day International debut in the 1975 World Cup?

19 Which West Indian smashed 35 runs from 10 consecutive Dennis Lillee deliveries?

20 Which assurance company sponsored the tournament?

Answers on page 208

1979 Cricket World Cup

1   Which country hosted the 1979 Cricket World Cup?

2   Who won the tournament?

3   Who were the runners-up?

4   True or false: the USA appeared in the 1979 Cricket World Cup?

5   Who hit 10 fours and three sixes while smashing 86 from just 66 deliveries in the final?

6   Who did England dismiss for just 45 in the group stage?

7   Which batsman scored an unbeaten 138 in the final?

8   Which pace bowler took five for 38 in the final?

9   Sri Lanka gained their maiden World Cup victory over which country: England, India or Pakistan?

10   Which 'chilly' England seamer took four for eight from 10 overs against Canada?

11   Which West Indian was the leading run scorer in the tournament: Gordon Greenidge, Viv Richards or Clive Lloyd?

12   Which Australian batsman played in the first of his four World Cups in 1979?

13   Who captained England in the tournament?

14 True or false: Ian Botham made his World Cup debut in 1979?

15 Matches in the 1979 World Cup were how many overs a side: 50, 55 or 60?

16 Which Englishman played in the first of his four World Cups in 1979?

17 What was the margin of victory in the final: 52 runs, 72 runs or 92 runs?

18 Which England batsman was an unlikely bowling hero taking two wickets against both Pakistan and Australia?

19 Which Englishman was the leading wicket taker in the 1979 World Cup?

20 How many sides took part in the competition: 8, 10 or 12?

Answers on page 208

QUIZ 6 1983 Cricket World Cup

1 Which country hosted the 1983 Cricket World Cup?

2 Who were the winners of the competition?

3 Who were the beaten finalists?

4 What was the highest individual score in the 1983 final: 38, 48 or 58?

5 Which renowned slow scorer opened the batting for England throughout the tournament?

6 Which member of the Zimbabwe squad later went on to play Test cricket for England?

7 Who smashed 175 not out from just 138 balls against Zimbabwe in their second match in June?

8 Which England seamer turned commentator went for 82 runs from his 12 overs against Sri Lanka?

9 New Zealand's Martin Sneddon had bowling figures of 12-1-105-2 against which country in their second match in June?

10 Who captained England in the competition?

11 Who was named Man of the Match in Zimbabwe's shock win over Australia?

12 Which Lancastrian opened the batting for England in the tournament?

Answers on page 208

13 Which Indian seamer was the leading wicket taker in the 1983 World Cup?

14 Which Pakistani leg spinner took four for 21 against New Zealand in their first match in June?

15 Which current umpire was England's wicketkeeper in 1983?

16 Which English born Australian took six for 39 in a group game against India?

17 Who scored 130 for England against Sri Lanka: David Gower, Graham Gooch or Ian Botham?

18 How many runs did India score in the final: 173, 183 or 193?

19 Which Indian seamer took three for 31 in the final?

20 Who was named as Man of the Match in the final?

Answers on page 208

QUIZ 7 1987 Cricket World Cup

1 Where was the 1987 Cricket World Cup held?

2 Matches were played with how many overs for each side: 50, 55 or 60?

3 Which team won the competition?

4 Who were the beaten finalists?

5 Which West Indian made the highest score in the tournament?

6 In the opening match Australia beat which team by just one run: India, Pakistan or Sri Lanka?

7 One captain unexpectedly dismissed his opposite number in the final. Who were the two players?

8 What feat was achieved for the first time in World Cup history by Chetan Sharma in 1987?

9 Which Englishman was the leading run scorer in the tournament?

10 Mike Gatting was dismissed in the final playing which infamous shot?

11 Which team posted the highest score of the tournament, a mammoth 360 for four against Sri Lanka?

12 Which Australian was the leading wicket taker in the competition?

13 England played two specialist spinners in the final. Who were they?

14 Who was Australia's wicketkeeper at the 1987 World Cup: Tim Zoehrer, Ian Healy or Greg Dyer?

15 Which city hosted the final of the 1987 World Cup?

16 Which England all rounder was smashed for 83 runs from 10 wicketless overs against the West Indies: Derek Pringle, Phil DeFreitas or David Capel?

17 Which Australian batsman won three Man of the Match awards?

18 Two West Indian born players played for England in the 1987 World Cup final. Phil DeFreitas was one, who was the other?

19 Two Australians who played in the 1987 World Cup also went on to play in the 1999 event. Who were they?

20 What was the winning margin in the final: 7 runs, 7 wickets or 77 runs?

1992 Cricket World Cup

1 True or false: the 1992 Cricket World Cup was the first where coloured clothing was worn?

2 Which two countries hosted the tournament?

3 Which country played in their first World Cup in 1992?

4 Which country won the tournament?

5 Who were the runners-up?

6 Which Zimbabwean chicken farmer was the Man of the Match in their group game against England?

7 Which former Worcestershire spinner opened the bowling for New Zealand?

8 Which England all rounder took one wicket for two runs from five overs in the group game against Pakistan?

9 Who took three wickets for eight runs in the same match?

10 Which team beat Pakistan by 10 wickets in the group stage?

11 Who took four wickets in seven balls without conceding a run during England's eight wicket rout of Australia?

12 Which New Zealander was named as Player of the Tournament?

Answers on page 209

13 India's Kiran More was involved in a dispute with which Pakistani during their group stage game?

14 Who was the leading wicket taker in the 1992 Cricket World Cup?

15 True or false: the 1992 World Cup was the first World Cup to feature matches played under floodlights?

16 How old was Imran Khan when he captained Pakistan in the final: 37, 38 or 39?

17 The 1992 World Cup Final was held at which ground?

18 Which Pakistani smashed a crucial 42 from just 35 balls in the final?

19 Who kept wicket for England in the competition?

20 In England's group game against New Zealand eight of their 11 were born outside England. Who were they?

Answers on page 209

1996 Cricket World Cup

1 Which three countries hosted the 1996 Cricket World Cup?

2 Which country won the tournament?

3 Who were the runners-up?

4 Which usually dour South African with 188 not out recorded the highest score of in the 1996 World Cup?

5 Which three countries made their World Cup debut in 1996?

6 Who was the only England player to hit a century in the competition: Michael Atherton, Alec Stewart or Graeme Hick?

7 Which two sides forefeited matches after refusing to play in Colombo?

8 Who knocked England out of the competition?

9 The West Indies were beaten by which cricketing minnows by 73 runs?

10 Which England off spinner won the Man of the Match award against UAE, despite being forced to leave the field after being violently sick?

11 What odds were Sri Lanka at the start of the competition: 20/1, 33/1 or 66/1?

12 Which Indian was the leading wicket taker in the 1996 World Cup?

13 Which New Zealander scored 130 in their match against Australia: Chris Harris, Chris Cairns or Nathan Astle?

14 The 1996 World Cup final was held in which city: Lahore, Karachi or Faisalabad?

15 Which Indian was the leading run scorer in the competition?

16 How many members of the UAE team were actually born in UAE: none, one or two?

17 Australia recovered from 15 for 4 to beat which team in the semi-final?

18 Who was named Man of the Match in the final of the 1996 World Cup after scoring an unbeaten 107?

19 Who was the England captain at the tournament?

20 Seven members of England's 1996 squad also played in the 1992 World Cup. Who were they?

Answers on page 209

QUIZ 10

1999 Cricket World Cup

1 Who won the 1999 Cricket World Cup?

2 Who were the beaten finalists?

3 Which of the following countries did not host a match in the 1999 World Cup: Ireland, Holland or France?

4 Which burly seamer played two matches for England and was on the winning side on both occasions?

5 Which two countries made their World Cup debut in 1999?

6 Which Indian batsman with 461 runs was the leading run scorer?

7 Which blonde American model was an 'ambassador' for the 1999 World Cup?

8 Which South African was said to have 'dropped the World Cup'?

9 True or false: the official World Cup anthem was released after England had already been knocked out of the competition?

10 Allan Donald was involved in a catastrophic run out with which all rounder in the semi-final against Australia?

11 Zimbabwe shocked which team to pip England to a place in the Super Sixes?

Answers on page 209

12 Pakistan were beaten by which minnow in the group stage?

13 Which Indian seamer turned coach took five for 27 against Pakistan in the Super Six stage: Prasad, Srinath or Ganguly?

14 Who did Pakistan face in the semi-final of the 1999 World Cup?

15 Which Indian smashed the highest score of the tournament, 183 against Sri Lanka?

16 Shane Warne shared the honour for leading wicket taker in the tournament with which New Zealander?

17 Who was Pakistan's top scorer in the final: Wasim Akram, Ijaz Ahmed or Extras?

18 Who with figures of four for 33 was named as Man of the Match in the final: Glenn McGrath, Shane Warne or Paul Reiffel?

19 Who captained England in the tournament: Alec Stewart, Nasser Hussain or Michael Atherton?

20 Who with 11 wickets was England's leading wicket taker?

Answers on page 209

QUIZ 11 2003 Cricket World Cup

1 The 2003 Cricket World Cup was primarily hosted in which country?

2 Which country won the competition?

3 Who were the runners-up?

4 What was the margin of victory in the final: 10 runs, 75 runs or 125 runs?

5 Which Zimbabwean made the highest individual score in the competition?

6 Which Indian was the leading run scorer in the 2003 Cricket World Cup?

7 Who was the tournament's leading wicket taker: Chaminda Vaas, Muttiah Muralitharan or Glen McGrath?

8 Which Australian took seven for 20 and scored a crucial 34 not out in Australia's two wicket win over England?

9 Canada were dismissed for just 36 by which team?

10 Which Canadian reached a century off just 67 balls against the West Indies?

11 Which four countries reached the semi-finals of the 2003 Cricket World Cup?

12 Which country refused to play in Kenya because of safety fears?

13 Which country refused to play in Zimbabwe because of fears for the players' safety?

14 The first bowler to take a five wicket haul in the tournament played for which unlikely country: Canada, Kenya or Namibia?

15 Kenya beat which three Test playing nations during the competition?

16 Who was the top scorer in the final?

17 South Africa were involved in a tie with which country in the group stage?

18 Kenya's Aasif Karim recorded the impressive figures of 8.2-6-7-3 against which country: Australia, Sri Lanka or New Zealand?

19 Which five Test playing nations failed to reach the Super Six stage of the competition?

20 The final was held in which city?

Answers on page 209

2007 Cricket World Cup

1   Where was the 2007 Cricket World Cup held?

2   Who won the competition?

3   Who were the runners-up?

4   The tournament was overshadowed by the death of which coach?

5   Pakistan suffered a shock defeat at the hands of which country: Ireland, Scotland or Holland?

6   Who was England's top scorer against both Kenya and Canada?

7   Who shocked India, beating them by five wickets in Group B?

8   Who scored 149 runs in the final?

9   Only three players took five wickets in an innings at the 2007 World Cup. They all played for the same country. Which one?

10   Who was the leading run scorer in the competition?

11   Who hit six sixes in an over in the group stage?

12   Who was the unfortunate bowler?

13   Zimbabwe were involved in a tied match against which side?

14 Which Sri Lankan took four wickets in four balls against South Africa and still ended up on the losing side?

15 Which umpire officiated in his fifth consecutive World Cup final?

16 Which two wicketkeepers broke the record for the fastest 50 in the World Cup?

17 Which burly Bermudan took a stunning one handed catch to dismiss Robin Uthappa in their game against India?

18 Who was named as the Man of the Tournament?

19 Which team became the first side to score more than 400 in a World Cup innings?

20 Who are the five players who played in both the 1992 and 2007 World Cups?

Answers on page 209

World Twenty20 2007

1 Which country hosted the inaugural World Twenty20?

2 Who won the competition?

3 Who were the runners-up?

4 Who was named as Man of the Match in the final?

5 Who with 13 wickets was the leading wicket taker in the 2007 World Twenty20: Umar Gul, Mohammad Asif or Yasir Arafat?

6 What was the margin of victory in the final: 5 runs, 15 runs or 50 runs?

7 Who did Australia face in the semi-final?

8 Which Australian took a hat-trick in their group game against Bangladesh: Stuart Clark, Brett Lee or Nathan Bracken?

9 Which two teams were involved in a bowl out in the group stage of the competition?

10 England won only one game in the whole tournament. Who did they beat?

11 Which Australian was the tournament's leading run scorer with 265?

12 Who was the only person to score a century in the 2007 Twenty20 World Cup?

13 Which Indian hit six sixes in an over?

14 Who was the unfortunate England bowler?

15 Which team compiled an impressive 260 for six against Kenya, the highest score in the tournament?

16 Which team scored the lowest total, managing just 83 against Sri Lanka?

17 Which Sri Lankan spinner conceded 64 from his allocation of four overs against Pakistan?

18 Which New Zealander produced the best bowling figures of four for seven against Kenya?

19 Who was the leading six hitter in the competition: Craig McMillan, Yuvraj Singh or Shahid Afridi?

20 Who hit the most sixes in a single innings?

Answers on page 210

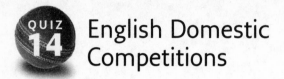

English Domestic Competitions

1 Which side won every County Championship from 1952 through to 1958?

2 Which county won the first two Sunday League titles?

3 In what year did the first Gillette Cup take place: 1963, 1973 or 1983?

4 Which county won the first Gillette Cup?

5 Who won the first Benson and Hedges Cup final in 1972?

6 Which county won the most Benson and Hedges Cup titles?

7 Which West Indian pacemen, with seven for 12 has the best bowling figures in the history of the Benson and Hedges Cup: Wayne Daniel, Sylvester Clarke or Malcolm Marshall?

8 Which county set a record total of 489 in their final match of the 2007 season to win the County Championship, ended up short by just 24 runs?

9 What is the lowest score in the final of the Natwest Trophy: 57, 77 or 97?

10 Alistair Brown scored 268 not out against which county in the 2002 Cheltenham & Gloucester Trophy?

11 Who won the Cheltenham & Gloucester Trophy in 2007?

12 Which side has won the County Championship the most times?

13 Which two counties have never won the Cheltenham & Gloucester/Natwest/Gillette Trophy?

14 Which county won the 2007 County Championship?

15 Which Somerset bowler once bowled eight consecutive maidens in a Sunday League game?

16 Which county hosted the first domestic day/night One Day game in England in 1997?

17 Which county won both the Natwest Trophy and the Benson and Hedges Cup in both 1999 and 2000?

18 Who were the two umpires in the last Benson and Hedges final who had also played against each other in the first Benson and Hedges final?

19 Which Somerset batsman hit a century from just 36 balls in the 1990 Natwest Trophy: Graham Rose, Ian Botham or Viv Richards?

20 Which 19 year old was the man of the match in the 1997 Benson and Hedges final after hitting 98 against Kent?

Answers on page 210

English Twenty20 Cup

1   Which county won the 2007 Twenty20 Cup?

2   Who were the runners-up?

3   Which South African born all rounder was Man of the Match in the 2007 final?

4   Which two counties were beaten in the semi-finals?

5   Which Northamptonshire all rounder with an unbeaten 111, posted the highest individual score in the 2007 Twenty20 Cup?

6   Which Sussex all rounder hit 19 sixes in the 2007 competition?

7   Which Indian spinner took five for 13 from his four overs in a game against Essex in 2007?

8   The highest score in the English Twenty20 Cup is 250 for three by which county: Somerset, Surrey or Sussex?

9   Which English county has recorded the two lowest domestic Twenty20 Cup scores?

10   Who are the only county to win the Twenty20 Cup twice?

11   Which big hitting Australian has posted the highest individual score in the Twenty20 Cup?

12   Which county won the first Twenty20 Cup in 2003?

13 Which Australian smashed a century off just 34 balls for Kent in 2004?

14 Yorkshire's Gerard Brophy holds the record for the fastest 50 in domestic Twenty20. How many balls did it take him: 14, 16 or 18?

15 Which Surrey seamer took six for 24 from his four overs against Middlesex in 2005?

16 Which usually reliable England seamer holds the record for the most runs conceded from a four over spell?

17 Which Hampshire all rounder had the remarkable figures of 3.5 overs 2 maidens 5 for 14 including a hat-trick against Sussex in 2004?

18 Which of the following haven't performed at Twenty20 Cup finals day: All Saints, Sugababes or Girls Aloud?

19 Which venue will host the 2008 Twenty20 Cup final?

20 Which Surrey, Essex and England all rounder has the best strike rate of any bowler in the Twenty20 Cup?

Answers on page 210

QUIZ 16 India versus Australia 2001

1 What was the score in the classic 2001 Test series between India and Australia?

2 What was the margin of victory in the first Test: Australia won by 10 wickets, Australia won by 10 runs or match drawn?

3 Who was fined half his match fee and given a one game ban (suspended for six months) after an on field altercation with umpire Venkat over a disputed catch?

4 Which Indian bowler took a hat-trick in the first innings of the second Test match in Kolkata?

5 India trailed Australia by how many runs after the first innings of the second Test: 74, 174 or 274?

6 Who topped scored with 110 in Australia's first innings in the second Test?

7 Who hit 281 in India's second innings in the second Test?

8 Which pair batted for the whole of the fourth day of the second Test, adding a record breaking 376 runs?

9 How many runs did India total in their second innings in Kolkata: 567, 657 or 756?

10 Who took six wickets in Australia's second innings claiming a total of 13 in the match?

11 Which unlikely Indian bowler dismissed Hayden, Gilchrist and Warne in the second innings of the Kolkata Test?

12 Which Australian made a double century in the first innings of the third Test in Chennai?

13 Who took 15 wickets and also hit the winning runs in the third Test?

14 What was India's margin of victory in Chennai: two wickets, two runs or 12 runs?

15 Which Australian batsman made 47 in both innings of the third Test and was out handled the ball in the first: Mark Waugh, Steve Waugh or Michael Slater?

16 Who took just 10 wickets at an average of over 50 during the series?

17 Which Australian scored 122 runs in his first innings in the series but then added only two more runs in his next four innings?

18 Harbhajan Singh took 32 wickets in the series. How many wickets did India's next leading wicket taker take?

19 Who was Australia's leading wicket taker in the series?

20 Who were the two captains during the series?

Answers on page 210

Sheffield Shield

1 How many teams compete for the Sheffield Shield?

2 Which state have won the competition the most times?

3 Which state first took part in the competition in 1977/78?

4 Since its inception in 1976, which player has won the Player of the Year award the most times?

5 Which food company has sponsored the competition since 1999?

6 Which former Yorkshire batsman has scored the most runs in the competition?

7 Which so called One Day specialist holds the record for the most runs in a Sheffield Shield season?

8 True or false: Don Bradman averaged 99.94 in Shield cricket?

9 Which 'funky' player holds the record for the most wickets in a season?

10 The Gabba is the home to which Australian state side?

11 In what year was the five day final between the top two sides introduced?

12 Which former Somerset captain holds the record for the most Sheffield Shield appearances?

13 Which well built Lancastrian spinner captained Tasmania on their Shield debut?

14 Which South African scored 325 in a day for South Australia against Western Australia in 1970/71?

15 What is the highest innings total in a Shield match: 903, 957 or 1,107?

16 Dennis Lillee, Justin Langer and John Inverarity all played for which state?

17 How many years did it take for Queensland to break their Shield duck: 16, 46 or 68 years?

18 Graham Thorpe is a batting coach at which Australian state side?

19 Which state won three consecutive Shields between 1999/00 and 2000/01?

20 Which state were bowled out for just 29 in 2004/05 with Nathan Bracken taking an amazing seven wickets for just four runs?

Answers on page 210

World Series Cricket

QUIZ 18

1 Who was the billionaire businessman behind World Series Cricket?

2 In what year did the first so called Supertest take place: 1976, 1977 or 1978?

3 Who was stripped of the England captaincy for his role in the affair?

4 Which three sides competed in World Series Cricket?

5 Who was the captain of the Australian side?

6 Which Englishman took to wearing a motorcycle helmet in light of the fearsome fast bowling?

7 Which Australian left-hander had his jaw broken by an Andy Roberts bouncer?

8 How many balls were there in a World Series Cricket over: 6, 8 or 10?

9 Which Australian took 79 wickets in the 14 Supertests?

10 What colour was the original ball used in the first day/night matches: yellow, white or orange?

11 Five South Africans played in World Series Cricket. Can you name them?

12 Which England wicketkeeper played for the Rest of the World side?

Answers on page 210

13 The first World Series Supertest was held at Waverley Park which usually hosted which sport: rugby union, Australian Rules football or football?

14 Who captained the West Indian side in World Series Cricket?

15 What revolutionary idea was used for the first time in the first WSC Supertest: a drop in pitch, a third TV umpire or a metal bat?

16 True or false: one of the the Supertests was held at a trotting track?

17 Which of the following didn't play World Series Cricket: Derek Underwood, Bob Woolmer or Geoff Boycott?

18 True or false: the West Indies wore a pink uniform in the One Day matches in World Series Cricket?

19 Which WSC advertising jingle was released as a single, reached number one and can still be heard in grounds today?

20 True or false: World Series Cricket matches still do not have First Class status?

Answers on page 210

QUIZ 19 Ambrose and Walsh

1 Curtly Ambrose is from which Caribbean island?

2 Which English county did Ambrose play for?

3 Courtney Walsh made his Test debut against which country: England, Australia or India?

4 Walsh holds the record for the most Test match ducks. How many did he make: 23, 33 or 43?

5 How many Test wickets did Ambrose and Walsh take in the 49 Tests they played together: 391, 451 or 491?

6 Walsh played domestic cricket for which English county?

7 Ambrose took seven wickets for just one run in an amazing spell against which country?

8 Which Australian batsman ill advisedly asked Ambrose to remove his sweatbands in a One Day International?

9 How many Test wickets did Courtney Walsh take?

10 True or false: Ambrose once bowled a 15 ball over containing nine no balls?

11 Which batsman did both Ambrose and Walsh dismiss the most times in Test cricket?

12 Ambrose bowled a pair of beamers at which Warwickshire player in 1990?

Answers on page 211

13 Who did Walsh succeed as West Indies captain in 1994?

14 True or false: Walsh plays in a reggae band called The Big Bad Dread and the Baldhead?

15 Ambrose took his Test best figures of 8-45 against which country?

16 Walsh played domestic cricket for which Caribbean island?

17 What are Ambrose's middle names?

18 How many Test wickets did Ambrose take?

19 In what year was Walsh named as a Wisden Cricketer of the Year: 1986, 1987 or 1988?

20 True or false: England were bowled out for just 46 runs in Ambrose's 46th Test match?

Answers on page 211

QUIZ 20 Allan Border

1 Allan Border won how many Test caps for Australia: 136, 146 or 156?

2 What was Border's highest Test score?

3 Allan Border played for which two English counties?

4 How many World Cups did Border appear in?

5 In what year did Border first captain the Australian Test team: 1984, 1985 or 1986?

6 Who did Border dismiss to claim his first Test wicket?

7 True or false: Border was run out for a duck in the second innings of his Test debut?

8 Who did Border replace as Australian Test captain?

9 How many times did Border take five wickets in an innings in a Test match?

10 Which Italian footballer, when asked who his childhood hero was, answered Allan Border?

11 Against which country did Border score his maiden Test century?

12 In what year did Border lift the World Cup?

13 Which Essex bowler was Border's last Test victim?

Answers on page 211

14 Border played most of his Australian domestic cricket for which state?

15 How many Test centuries did Border score: 25, 26 or 27?

16 Border was the first player to achieve what feat in a Test match: 150 in each innings or double century and 10 wickets in a match?

17 Where did Border play his last Test innings: Durban, Cape Town or Johannesburg?

18 True or false: Border never won a Test series against the West Indies?

19 How many times did Border captain Australia: 73, 83 or 93?

20 What is Border's nickname?

Answers on page 211

Sir Ian Botham

1 Ian Botham played for which three English counties?

2 Botham made his Test debut against which country?

3 How many did Botham score in the second innings of the famous Headingley Test of 1981?

4 Botham played professional football for which team?

5 Botham holds the record for the most Test wickets taken by an Englishman. How many did he take?

6 Which Australian bowler did Botham hit for 22 runs in a single over in the 1986/87 Ashes?

7 Who did Botham dismiss to claim his first Test match wicket: Ian Chappell, Greg Chappell or Trevor Chappell?

8 In 1980, Botham became the first player to do what in a Test match: take 10 wickets and score a century or take 10 catches?

9 Botham had a spell with which Australian state side?

10 Botham is famous for advertising which breakfast cereal?

11 What is Botham's middle name: Toby, Thomas or Terence?

12 What is Botham's highest Test score?

13 True or false: Botham never made a One Day International century?

14 How many matches did Botham win as England captain: none, four or eight?

15 Botham was a captain on which BBC quiz show?

16 Which county colleague dismissed Botham the most times in Test cricket?

17 Botham's best Test bowling figures of eight for 34 came against which country?

18 Why was Botham suspended from cricket in the mid-1980s?

19 In what year did Botham win Sports Personality of the Year: 1980, 1981 or 1982?

20 True or false: Botham holds a helicopter pilot licence?

Geoffrey Boycott

1 Geoff Boycott played for which English county?

2 Boycott scored a rapid fire 146 in the 1965 Gillette Cup final against which county: Lancashire, Sussex or Surrey?

3 True or false: Boycott faced the first ball in One Day International cricket?

4 How many Test match centuries did Boycott compile: 18, 20 or 22?

5 Boycott was left stranded on 99 not out against which country in 1979/80?

6 Boycott reached his 100th First Class century by hitting which bowler for four: Ian Chappell, Greg Chappell or Trevor Chappell?

7 True or false: Boycott was once dropped by England despite scoring a double century in the previous match?

8 Which England colleague deliberately ran Boycott out in a Test match in New Zealand in 1978?

9 How many different opening partners did Boycott have for England: 12, 14 or 16?

10 Who was Boycott's most regular opening partner for England: Graham Gooch, John Edrich or Dennis Amiss?

Answers on page 211

11 Boycott took seven Test wickets including which left-handed South African great?

12 Which chat show host played alongside Boycott for Barnsley Cricket Club?

13 How old was Boycott when he scored his final Test century?

14 Boycott was involved in a run out with which Nottinghamshire batsman at the Trent Bridge Test in 1977?

15 Boycott is a fan of which football team: Manchester United, Barnsley or Sheffield Wednesday?

16 Which all rounder did Boycott famously describe as a 'show pony' in a live TV interview in 1996?

17 What is Boycott's nickname: Fiery, Grizzly or Deadly?

18 What was Boycott's final Test match batting average: 42.58, 44.25 or 47.72?

19 How many times did Boycott average over 100 in an English First Class season: never, once or twice?

20 Boycott briefly played for which South African province?

Answers on page 211

Sir Donald Bradman

1 How many Test matches did Don Bradman play for Australia: 52, 72 or 92?

2 What was Bradman's highest Test score: 234, 284 or 334?

3 Bradman scored 309 not out in a day at which English ground in 1930?

4 True or false: Bradman was never dismissed in the nineties in a Test match?

5 What was Bradman's final Test batting average?

6 Who dismissed Bradman for nought in his final Test innings?

7 Which two Australian state sides did Bradman play for?

8 Which actor, best known for playing Elrond in *The Lord Of The Rings* trilogy, played Bradman's nemesis Douglas Jardine in the TV series *Bodyline*?

9 True or false: Bradman is the only player to score two Test match triple centuries?

10 Bradman holds the record for the most runs in a Test series. How many runs did he make against England in 1930: 774, 874 or 974?

11 How many Test wickets did Bradman take: two, seven or nine?

Answers on page 211

12 How old was Bradman when he led the Australian 'Invincibles' to victory in the 1948 Ashes: 37, 38 or 39?

13 Bradman holds the record for the most Test match double centuries. How many did he score?

14 What was Bradman's middle name: George, Gregory or Geoffrey?

15 In what year was Bradman knighted: 1949, 1959 or 1969?

16 True of false: Bradman scored a century in 36% of his 80 Test innings?

17 True or false: Australia lost by 675 runs on Bradman's Test debut?

18 Which ill-fated Yorkshire spinner dismissed Bradman the most times in his Test career?

19 What did Bradman famously say after watching Stan McCabe score a double century against England in 1938?

20 What was Bradman's highest First Class score: 334, 399 or 452 not out?

Answers on page 211

Andrew Flintoff

1 Andrew Flintoff plays for which county?

2 Flintoff made his Test debut against which country in 1998?

3 Flintoff gets his nickname from which cartoon character: Fred Flintstone, Barney Rubble or Henry's Cat?

4 Which all rounder did Flintoff dismiss to claim his first Test wicket?

5 Flintoff's maiden Test century came against which country?

6 How many sixes did Flintoff hit in the 2005 Ashes Test at Edgbaston: seven, eight or nine?

7 Flintoff was disciplined in the 2007 World Cup after an incident involving what form of transport: a canoe, a pedalo or a surfboard?

8 Which Surrey bowler was smashed for 34 runs in an over by Flintoff in 1998?

9 True or false: Flintoff won the Beard Liberation Front's Beard of the Year Award in 2004 and 2005?

10 What is Flintoff's highest Test score: 157, 167 or 177?

11 Flintoff added 99 runs in a ninth wicket partnership with Steve Harmison against South Africa in 2003. How many runs did Harmison contribute to the partnership?

12 Which former Lancashire left-hander is Flintoff's manager?

13 Flintoff took five wickets during a marathon spell at which ground during the 2005 Ashes?

14 Which West Indian did Flintoff advise to 'mind the windows' at Lord's in 2004?

15 True or false: Flintoff batted on all five days of a Test match in India in 2006?

16 Which bowler dismissed Flintoff in his maiden Test innings?

17 What is Flintoff's middle name?

18 In what year was Flintoff named BBC Sports Personality of the Year?

19 How many runs did Flintoff score in the 2005 Ashes series: 202, 302 or 402?

20 How old was Flintoff when he made his Test debut: 19, 20 or 21?

Answers on page 211

QUIZ 25 Brian Lara

1 Brian Lara is from which Caribbean island: Jamaica, Antigua or Trinidad?

2 Lara played cricket for which English county?

3 Who did Lara make his Test debut against?

4 Lara scored 277 against which country in 1993?

5 Who did Lara overtake to become the leading Test run scorer of all time?

6 Lara is a close friend of which former Aston Villa and Manchester United Premiership footballer?

7 True or false: Lara scored six centuries in seven innings while at Warwickshire?

8 How many Test match double centuries did Lara score in his career: seven, eight or nine?

9 Lara broke the highest individual Test score record in 1994 by hitting which bowler for four: Angus Fraser, Chris Lewis or Andrew Caddick?

10 True or false: Lara scored a century against every Test playing nation?

11 Brian Lara scored 400 not out in a Test against which country?

12 Lara has an honorary degree from which English University: Exeter, Warwick or Birmingham?

13 Lara holds the record for the highest ever First Class score. How many runs did he make?

14 Who were the opposition when Lara broke the highest First Class score record?

15 Lara had a short spell playing for which South African province?

16 What is Lara's middle name: Courtney, Charles or Christopher?

17 Which player dismissed Lara the most times in Test cricket?

18 What was Lara's final Test match batting average: 49.89, 50.89 or 52.89?

19 Who did Lara succeed in his first spell as West Indies captain in 1996?

20 Lara scored 28 runs from an over bowled by which South African spinner in a Test match in 2003?

QUIZ 26 Lillee and Thomson

1 How many Test wickets did Dennis Lillee take: 345, 355 or 365?

2 True or false: Thomson played his first Test match with a broken bone in his foot?

3 Which English wicketkeeper did Lillee dismiss most often in his Test career?

4 Who did Thomson dismiss most in Test cricket?

5 Lillee played for which two Australian state sides?

6 How many Test wickets did Thomson take: 150, 200 or 250?

7 Lillee had a short spell at which English county?

8 How many wickets did Thomson take in the 1974/75 series against England: 23, 27 or 33?

9 How many times did 'caught Marsh bowled Lillee' appear on Test scorecards: 75, 85 or 95?

10 Thomson played in the English County Championship for which side?

11 Which English opener did Lillee dismiss to claim his maiden Test wicket: Geoff Boycott, Dennis Amiss or John Edrich?

12 True or false: Thomson was wicketless on his Test debut?

13 How many Test match caps did Lillee win: 70, 85 or 100?

14 Which England batsman was hit in the unmentionables by a Thomson delivery in 1974/75?

15 What was Lillee's highest Test score: 43 not out, 53 not out or 73 not out?

16 Lillee runs a pace academy in which Indian city?

17 True or false: Thomson was immortalised in the song '*No Reservations*' by Men At Work?

18 Lillee was involved in an unseemly clash with which Pakistani in 1981?

19 Which Englishman became Thomson's last Test victim in 1985: David Gower, Graham Gooch or Ian Botham?

20 What is Lillee's middle name: Keith, Kevin or Kenneth?

Answers on page 212

Muttiah Muralitharan

1 Muttiah Muralitharan plays for which country: India, Pakistan or Sri Lanka?

2 In what year did Murali make his Test debut: 1992, 1993 or 1994?

3 Which Australian fast bowler did Murali dismiss to claim his first Test wicket?

4 Murali was no-balled for throwing in a Test match by which controversial Australian umpire?

5 Murali has played for which two English counties?

6 True or false: Murali is the only player to take nine wickets in a Test innings twice?

7 Who did Murali overtake to become the all time leading Test wicket taker in May 2004?

8 He claimed his 700th Test wicket against which country?

9 Which South African wicketkeeper has Murali dismissed the most times in his Test career?

10 Murali recorded his best Test match figures of 16 for 220 against which country?

11 How many World Cup finals has Murali appeared in?

12 What is Murali's highest Test score: 17, 37 or 67?

Answers on page 212

13 Which Australian captain described Murali as 'the Don Bradman of bowling'?

14 Murali took nine wickets in an innings against England in 1998. Who was the only batsman he didn't dismiss: John Crawley, Alec Stewart or Ian Salisbury?

15 How many wickets did Murali take in the 2007 World Twenty20: none, five or 10?

16 True or false: Murali took 10 wickets in a match in four consecutive Test matches in 2006?

17 Which England batsman famously reverse swept Murali for six at Edgbaston in 2006?

18 How many wickets did Murali take in the 2007 World Cup: 19, 21 or 23?

19 True or false: Murali once dressed up in lederhosen to promote a Lancashire floodlit game?

20 Which Australian prime minister accused Murali of being a chucker?

Answers on page 212

QUIZ 28 Kevin Pietersen

1 Kevin Pietersen was born in which country?

2 Against which country did Pietersen make his Test debut?

3 How many runs did he make in his first Test innings: 0, 37 or 57?

4 Pietersen started his English career at which county?

5 How many centuries did Pietersen score in his first 30 Test matches?

6 True or false: Pietersen has been dismissed for 154 three times in his Test career?

7 Pietersen recorded his highest Test score of 226 against which side?

8 Which wicketkeeper did Pietersen dismiss to claim his first Test wicket?

9 Pietersen's wife was a singer in which band: Liberty X, Spice Girls or Sugababes?

10 How many catches did Pietersen drop in the 2005 Ashes series?

11 How many centuries did Pietersen score in the One Day series against South Africa in 2005: one, two or three?

Answers on page 212

12 Pietersen shared a record breaking partnership of 310 with which batsman at the Adelaide Test in 2006?

13 Which Sri Lankan did Pietersen reverse sweep for six at Edgbaston in 2006?

14 True or false: Pietersen was the only England player to score a century in the 2007 World Cup?

15 Which county did Pietersen join in 2004?

16 What is Pietersen's highest ODI score: 106, 116 or 126?

17 Who fractured Pietersen's rib in a One Day match against Australia in 2007?

18 How many First Class matches did Pietersen play for Hampshire in 2006?

19 Pietersen made his ODI debut against which country?

20 True or false: only Donald Bradman has scored more Test runs than Pietersen from his first 25 Test matches?

Answers on page 212

QUIZ 29 Sir Viv Richards

1 Sir Viv Richards is from which island in the Caribbean?

2 Against which side did Richards make his Test debut?

3 Richards scored 138 not out in the final of the Cricket World Cup in what year: 1975, 1979 or 1983?

4 Richards holds the record for the fastest Test century. How many balls did it take him?

5 What is Viv Richards' full name?

6 In what year did he receive his knighthood?

7 Richards played for Somerset and which other county?

8 How many times did Richards captain the West Indies in a Test match: 30, 40 or 50?

9 True or false: West Indies never lost a Test series when Richards was captain?

10 Which Australian batsman did Richards dismiss the most times in his Test career?

11 True or false: Richards played football in the qualifying rounds of the 1974 Football World Cup?

12 What was Richards' highest Test score?

13 Richards had a short spell playing for which Australian state side: NSW, Tasmania or Queensland?

14 What was Richards' highest One Day International score?

15 How many Test match centuries did Richards make: 20, 22 or 24?

16 In what year did Richards score 1,710 Test match runs?

17 Which England fast bowler was the last bowler to dismiss Richards in a Test match?

18 True or false: Richards appeared on a postage stamp in 2000?

19 Which Australian paceman dismissed Richards the most times in Test cricket?

20 True or false: Richards was voted one of Wisden's Five Cricketers of the 20th Century?

Answers on page 212

Sir Garfield Sobers

1 Did Sir Garfield bat and bowl left or righted?

2 Sobers is from which Caribbean island?

3 How old was Sobers when he made his Test debut: 17, 19 or 21?

4 What was Sobers' highest Test score?

5 Sobers played for which English county between 1968 and 1974?

6 True or false: Sobers had a batting average of nought in ODI cricket?

7 In what town did Sobers hit six sixes in an over: Cardiff, Swansea or Colwyn Bay?

8 How many Test wickets did Sobers take: 135, 235 or 335?

9 Who did Sobers succeed as West Indies captain: Everton Weekes, Frank Worrell or Clyde Walcott?

10 In what year did Garry become Sir Garry: 1975, 1985 or 1995?

11 How many Test match centuries did Sobers score: 16, 21 or 26?

12 What is Sobers' middle name: St Aubrun, St Anselm or St Anthony?

Answers on page 212

13 Sobers had a spell with which Australian state side?

14 How many Test caps did Sobers win: 83, 93 or 103?

15 True or false: Sobers was the first player to appear on a postage stamp?

16 What was Sobers' Test match batting average: 37.78, 47.78 or 57.78?

17 Who succeeded Sobers as West Indies captain in 1972?

18 Which England spinner dismissed Sobers in his final Test innings in 1974?

19 Which wicketkeeper did Sobers dismiss to claim his final Test wicket?

20 True or false: Sobers wrote a novel called 'Bonaventure and the Flashing Blade'?

Answers on page 212

Sachin Tendulkar

1 How old was Sachin Tendulkar when he made his Test debut: 16, 17 or 18?

2 Tendulkar was the first overseas player to play for which English county?

3 In 1988 Tendulkar put on an unbeaten 664 in a school game with which future Indian international?

4 Which Pakistani paceman dismissed Tendulkar in his first Test innings?

5 Tendulkar scored his maiden Test century against which country?

6 How old was he when he scored his first Test century: 16, 17 or 18?

7 True or false: Tendulkar was the first player to be given out Run out by the third umpire?

8 Tendulkar made his highest Test score of 248 not out against which country?

9 True or false: Tendulkar owns two restaurants?

10 True or false: Tendulkar didn't score his first One Day International century until his 79th match?

11 It took Tendulkar how many matches before he scored his first ODI century: 3, 45 or 79?

Answers on page 212

12 Who did Tendulkar succeed as Indian Test captain?

13 Tendulkar wears the same pads as which former Indian opener?

14 Which tennis player was Tendulkar's childhood idol?

15 Which fearsome Australian did Tendulkar dismiss to claim his first Test wicket?

16 In what year was Tendulkar named as one of Wisden's Five Cricketers of the Year: 1996, 1997 or 1998?

17 True or false: Tendulkar has never scored an international century at Lord's?

18 Tendulkar's Test best bowling figures of three for 10 came against which country?

19 Tendulkar was the top run scorer in which two World Cups?

20 True or false: Tendulkar is ambidextrous?

Answers on page 212

QUIZ 32   Michael Vaughan

1   Michael Vaughan plays domestic cricket for which English county?

2   Vaughan made his Test debut against which country?

3   What was the score when he faced his first ball in Test cricket: two for four, 50 for one or 100 for two?

4   Who did Vaughan replace as England captain?

5   Vaughan dismissed which Indian legend in the 2003 Trent Bridge Test?

6   What is Vaughan's highest Test score: 166, 183 or 197?

7   True or false: in 90 One Day Internationals Vaughan never made a century?

8   Vaughan is a fan of which Yorkshire football team: Sheffield United, Sheffield Wednesday or Leeds?

9   In what year did Vaughan score a record breaking 1,481 runs?

10   How many centuries did Vaughan make in the 2005 Ashes series?

11   Which unlikely bowler dismissed Vaughan at Trent Bridge in the 2005 Ashes?

12   Vaughan scored 633 in a series against which country in 2002/03?

13 England won eight Test matches in a row in 2004 under Vaughan's leadership against which three sides?

14 Whose record did Vaughan beat when he became the England captain with the most Test wins?

15 Vaughan scored centuries in both innings of the 2004 Lord's Test against which opposition?

16 In what year did Vaughan resign the England One Day captaincy?

17 What is Vaughan's nickname: Brains, Virgil or Joe 90?

18 Vaughan scored his maiden Test century against which country?

19 True or false: Vaughan's highest Test score against Zimbabwe is just 20?

20 Vaughan was named as one of Wisden's Five Cricketers of the Year in what year: 2002, 2003 or 2004?

Answers on page 212

Shane Warne

1 Which Indian did Shane Warne dismiss to claim his first Test wicket?

2 How many Test wickets did Warne take: 508, 608 or 708?

3 Warne dismissed which English batsman with the so called 'ball of the century'?

4 Which spinner has dismissed Warne the most in Test cricket?

5 Warne plays for which English county?

6 Which Englishman has Warne dismissed the most in Test matches?

7 What is Warne's highest Test score: 49, 79 or 99?

8 How many Test wickets did Warne take in 2005: 56, 76 or 96?

9 Warne has the same middle name as which Australian bowling legend?

10 How many World Cup finals did Warne appear in?

11 Warne took a hat-trick against England in 1994: DeFreitas and Gough were the first two victims, who was the third?

12 Warne is a huge fan of which Australian Rules Football team: Hawthorn, Essendon or St Kilda?

13 Which Englishman did Warne dismiss to claim his final Test wicket?

14 True or false: Warne has never captained Australia in a One Day International?

15 Warne played for which Australian state side?

16 True or false: Warne once appeared in *Neighbours*?

17 Warne's best bowling figures of 8-71 came against which team?

18 Who does Warne rate as the best batsman he has played against?

19 How many Test match half centuries did Warne score: none, 6 or 12?

20 Warne was sent a pallet of which food on the 1998 tour to India?

Answers on page 212

Wasim and Waqar

1 In what year and against which team did Wasim make his Test debut?

2 Who took more Test wickets, Wasim or Waqar?

3 Which county did Wasim spend the majority of his county career with?

4 True or false: Waqar was nicknamed the Rawalpindi Express?

5 How many Test match centuries did Wasim score: two, three or four?

6 Who was the leading wicket taker in the 1992 Cricket World Cup?

7 Waqar played for which two counties in the County Championship?

8 In what year was Waqar named as one of Wisden's Five Cricketers of the Year: 1991, 1992 or 1993?

9 What was Wasim's highest Test score: 127, 177 or 257 not out?

10 In what year did Wasim retire from international cricket?

11 In what year was Wasim named one of Wisden's Five Cricketers of the Year?

Answers on page 213

12 In what year was Waqar the County Championship leading wicket taker: 1993, 1995 or 1997?

13 Which legendary batsman described Wasim as 'the most outstanding bowler I've ever faced'?

14 Wasim took two Test match hat-tricks against which team?

15 True or false: Wasim holds the record for the highest Test score made by a number eight?

16 What was Waqar's highest Test score: 45, 65 or 85?

17 Which Indian was Waqar's first Test match victim?

18 True or false: Wasim took more than 500 One Day International wickets?

19 Wasim took three crucial wickets in the 1992 World Cup final. Who were the victims?

20 Which England left-hander was Wasim's final Test victim: Nick Knight, Graham Thorpe or Mark Butcher?

Answers on page 213

Australia

1 What colour is the famous cap worn by the Australian team in Test matches?

2 Who made 151 on his Test debut in India in 2004?

3 Which current Australian bowler has an alternative career as a suit salesman?

4 Who took 16 wickets on his Test debut at Lord's in 1972 but played only five further Test matches?

5 Who is the only Australian to score two Test match triple centuries?

6 Which Australian opener holds the record for the most Test dismissals in the nineties: Michael Slater, Justin Langer or Matthew Hayden?

7 What colour kit do Australia traditionally wear in One Day cricket?

8 Which Australian holds the record for the most Test match wickets in a calendar year?

9 Mark Taylor took one Test wicket in his career. Who was the unfortunate Pakistani batsman: Rashid Latif, Wasim Akram or Inzamam-ul-Haq?

10 Which former Australian all rounder once held the World Record for haggis throwing?

11 Australia recorded their highest ever Test score of 758 for eight against which side?

12 What is the highest Test score by an Australian and who scored it?

13 Don Bradman scored Test centuries in how many consecutive Test matches: four, five or six?

14 Who is Australia's all time leading Test wicket taker?

15 Which current Australian player is known as 'Mr Cricket'?

16 Who has played the most Test matches for Australia: Steve Waugh, Allan Border or Shane Warne?

17 Australia have been involved in two tied Test matches. Who were their opponents?

18 Australia suffered their first ever 10 wicket defeat in a One Day International to which opposition in 2007?

19 Which Australian captain carried a red handkerchief in his left pocket as a lucky charm?

20 In which Australian city is the Boxing Day Test match traditionally held?

Answers on page 213

Bangladesh

1   What is the nickname of the Bangladesh team: Lions, Tigers or Elephants?

2   In what year did Bangladesh make their Test match debut: 1999, 2000 or 2001?

3   Who was the first Bangladesh player to score a Test match century?

4   In what year did Bangladesh make their World Cup debut?

5   Which side did they famously defeat in the group stage of that World Cup?

6   How many Test matches did Bangladesh play before earning their first victory: 15, 25 or 35?

7   Who were Bangladesh's first Test match opponents?

8   Who did Bangladesh beat to claim their first Test win?

9   The highest score by a Bangladesh batsman in a Test match is 158 not out. Who scored it?

10 Who is the only Bangledesh bowler to take 10 wickets in a Test match?

11 Which team dismissed Bangladesh for just 62 in a Test match in 2007?

Answers on page 213

12 Which spinner had match figures of nine for 160 in a Test against Australia in 2006?

13 Which two Test playing nations did Bangladesh defeat in the 2007 World Cup?

14 Bangladesh beat which two sides in the 2007 World Twenty20?

15 Which Australian coached Bangladesh at the 2007 World Cup?

16 True or false: Bangladesh beat Australia in a One Day International in Cardiff in the run-up to the 2005 Ashes series?

17 Who smashed a half century off just 20 balls against the West Indies in the 2007 World Twenty20?

18 Mohammad Ashraful scored three of his first four Test centuries against which country?

19 Bangladesh played two Test matches in England in 2005. Lord's was one venue what was the other?

20 Which West Indian opening batsman coached Bangladesh between 1997 and 1999 and was made an honorary citizen of Bangladesh on his departure?

Answers on page 213

England

1   Who did Michael Vaughan replace as England Test captain in 2003?

2   Who is England's all time leading Test run scorer: Geoff Boycott, Graham Gooch or David Gower?

3   Who is England's most capped Test player?

4   Who replaced Michael Vaughan as England One Day captain in 2007?

5   Which England left-hander scored 21 One Day International fifties but never reached three figures?

6   Who with 99 not out against New Zealand in 1999, made England's highest score by a nightwatchman?

7   Which unlikely bowler was called for throwing at the Nottingham Test match in 1986?

8   Which Yorkshireman is the only living cricketer to have a pub named after him: Geoff Boycott, Darren Gough or Raymond Illingworth?

9   Which Yorkshire and England legend is the only man to be given out obstructing the field in a Test match?

10 Who played 71 Test matches between 1997 and 2004 but didn't appear in a single One Day International?

11 Who is the only England player of the last 50 years to have a surname ending in i?

12 Who is England's all time leading Test wicket taker: Ian Botham, Bob Willis or Fred Trueman?

13 Five England players scored centuries against the West Indies at Lord's in 2007. Who were they?

14 What do Alan Wells, Mike Watkinson, Kim Barnett and Colin Cowdrey have in common?

15 Which England seamer was named as Man of the Match in two of his three Test match appearances, all of which came in 2003?

16 What did England finally achieve after 585 attempts in the Ashes series of 1989?

17 Which England captain was the first person to be knighted for services to cricket?

18 Which former England seamer with 234 Test wickets is a qualified helicopter pilot?

19 Who holds the record for the most Test wins as England captain: Michael Atherton, Peter May or Michael Vaughan?

20 Who are the eight England cricketers to have won one hundred Test caps?

Answers on page 213

India

1 What colour kit do India wear in One Day Internationals?

2 Who led India to victory in the 2007 World Twenty20?

3 Who is the only Indian to score a Test match triple century?

4 In what decade did India play their first Test match: 1920s, 1930s or 1940s?

5 Which Indian medium pacer bowled the first ever delivery in the Cricket World Cup in 1975?

6 Which spinner took India's first Test hat-trick against Australia in 2001?

7 Who is India's all time leading Test wicket taker?

8 Which three Indians played for the ICC World XI in the Supertest against Australia in 2005?

9 Wicketkeeper Farokh Engineer played for which English county?

10 Who holds the record for the highest score by an Indian in a One Day International: Kapil Dev, Sachin Tendulkar or Mahendra Singh Dhoni?

11 Sunil Gavaskar took only one Test wicket. Which bespectacled Pakistani did he dismiss?

Answers on page 213

12 In what year did India claim their maiden Test victory in England: 1961, 1971 or 1981?

13 True or false: Vinoo Mankad batted at all 11 positions in Test matches for India?

14 Which Indian legend was David Gower's only Test match victim: Sunil Gavaskar, Kapil Dev or Bishen Bedi?

15 True or false: India have never lost a World Cup match against Pakistan?

16 Which Indian spinner took more Test wickets (242) than scored runs (167)?

17 Which Indian batsman who played in the 1983 World Cup Final, added an extra K to his surname so that it became nine letters long which is considered lucky in numerology?

18 Eden Gardens can be found in which Indian city?

19 Which Indian batsman has been dubbed Lord Snooty by some of his critics?

20 Who holds the record for the most Test dismissals by an Indian wicketkeeper: Syed Kirmani, Farokh Engineer or Kiran More?

Answers on page 213

QUIZ 39 New Zealand

1 What colour kit did New Zealand wear in the 1992 World Cup: beige, grey or black?

2 Which New Zealander took a hat-trick on his Test debut at the age of 34 against Pakistan in 1976?

3 How many times have New Zealand reached the semi-final of the Cricket World Cup: three, four or five times?

4 New Zealand have never won a Test series against which country?

5 In what decade were New Zealand granted Test status: 1930s, 1940s or 1950s?

6 In what year did the Kiwis gain their first Test match win over England: 1968, 1978 or 1988?

7 Which Kiwi great had a highest Test score of 299?

8 Who is the only New Zealander to make centuries in consecutive One Day Internationals: Lou Vincent, Mark Greatbatch or Chris Cairns?

9 Who is New Zealand's all time leading Test wicket taker?

10 Which all rounder, at six feet seven inches, is the tallest man to play for New Zealand?

11 Which New Zealand bowler shares a name with the singer from the band Coldplay?

Answers on page 213

12 Nathan Astle put on an unbeaten 106 for the last wicket with which unlikely partner to prevent an England victory in 1996?

13 How old was Daniel Vettori when he made his Test debut: 17, 18 or 19?

14 Who are the three New Zealand bowlers to have taken 200 Test wickets?

15 New Zealand were dismissed for the lowest ever Test score in 1955. How many did they make: 25, 26 or 27?

16 How many years did it take for New Zealand to win their first Test series: 20, 30 or 40?

17 Who are the two New Zealanders to take 200 One Day International wickets?

18 Which New Zealand batsman played in more that 40 Tests and averaged over 40 but never played on the winning side?

19 Which New Zealander holds the record for longest time taken to score nought?

20 In which city would you find the Jade Stadium?

Answers on page 213

QUIZ 40 Pakistan

1 What colour kit do Pakistan usually wear in One Day Internationals?

2 In what decade did Pakistan gain Test status: 1940s, 1950s or 1960s?

3 Which Australian Test bowler was appointed coach of Pakistan in July 2007?

4 Which Pakistani batsman holds the record for the most Test runs scored in a calendar year?

5 Pakistan's most famous supporter is known as: Father Cricket, Brother Cricket or Uncle Cricket?

6 Who are the three Pakistani batsmen to score 6,000 Test match runs?

7 Which spinner took 10 wickets in a Test match on four separate occasions against England in the 1980s?

8 Who hit the last ball of a One Day International against India for a match winning six in Sharjah in 1986?

9 Which Pakistani holds the record for the highest individual score in a One Day International?

10 Who are the three Pakistani bowlers to take a hat-trick in a Test match?

11 True or false: Pakistan have never won a Test series in the West Indies?

Answers on page 214

12 Which bespectacled Pakistani batsman was the first player to score centuries in three consecutive One Day Internationals?

13 Imran Khan captained Pakistan in how many Test matches: 28, 38 or 48?

14 Who are the two Pakistani batsmen to score Test match triple centuries?

15 Pakistan were dismissed in a Test match for 53 and 59 against which opposition in 2002?

16 Which two Pakistanis scored a century in their 100th Test match?

17 Pakistan recorded their first Test series win in England in what year: 1984, 1987 or 1990?

18 Pakistan have reached the final of the Cricket World Cup in which two years?

19 Who is Pakistan's all time leading Test wicket taker?

20 Pakistan were dismissed for their lowest ever One Day International total of 43 by which team in 1993?

Answers on page 214

South Africa

QUIZ 41

1 What colour kit do South Africa wear in One Day Internationals?

2 In what decade did South Africa make their One Day International debut: 1970s, 1980s or 1990s?

3 Which South African scored his 25th and 26th Test centuries against Pakistan in October 2007?

4 Who broke the record for most dismissals by a wicketkeeper in Test history in the same game?

5 True or false: South Africa won the gold medal for cricket in the Commonwealth Games in 1998?

6 When did South Africa play their first Test match: 1889, 1899 or 1909?

7 How many times have South Africa reached the final of the Cricket World Cup?

8 Who in 2006 became the first non-white player to captain South Africa in a Test match?

9 Who are the three South African bowlers to take three hundred Test wickets?

10 When Shane Warne said 'I've been waiting three and a half years for you to come back' which South African replied, 'It looks like you've spent the time eating'?

11 Which South African batsman had a Test match batting average of 60.97?

12 The South African team has which flower-related nickname?

13 In which city would you find The Wanderers?

14 Which South African was at number 11 in a TV poll to find the 100 Greatest South Africans?

15 Why don't South African players wear the number five shirt in One Day Internationals?

16 Which English county were known as 'Proctershire' in light of Mike Procter's immense performances at the club?

17 Who are the three South Africans to have scored 6,000 Test match runs?

18 Which South African has taken the most 10 wicket hauls in Test matches: Allan Donald, Shaun Pollock or Makhaya Ntini?

19 Who captained South Africa on their reintroduction to international cricket in 1992?

20 How old was Graham Smith when he became South Africa's youngest captain in 2003: 22, 23 or 24?

Answers on page 214

Sri Lanka

1 What colour kit do Sri Lanka wear in One Day International matches?

2 Sri Lanka's coach shares a name with the person who invented the wind-up radio. What is his name?

3 W.P.U.J.C. are the initials of which Sri Lankan seam bowler?

4 Which Sri Lankan holds the record for the most ducks in One Day International history?

5 In which year did Sri Lanka play their first Test match: 1972, 1982 or 1992?

6 Who is Sri Lanka's all time leading Test and One Day International wicket taker?

7 Who are the three Sri Lankans to score over 6,000 Test match runs?

8 Which Sri Lankan batsman scored only one run in his first six Test innings but went on to score 16 Test centuries?

9 Who holds the record for the best bowling figures in a One Day International of eight for 19?

10 Who is the only Sri Lankan to take a Test match hat-trick?

11 Which Sri Lankan was voted the Sexiest Man of the 2007 World Cup?

Answers on page 214

12 Mahela Jayawardene was involved in a mammoth partnership of 624 against South Africa with which batsman?

13 Which versatile batsman turned commentator had the nickname Rusty?

14 Which batsman was the first man to score identical Test centuries when he scored 105 in both innings against India in 1982: Duleep Mendis, Brendon Kuruppu or Arjuna Ranatunga?

15 Which Sri Lankan spinner went on to become a respected Test umpire?

16 Who led Sri Lanka to victory in the 1996 Cricket World Cup?

17 In which town would you find the R. Premadasa Stadium: Colombo, Galle or Dambulla?

18 Which Sri Lankan player is a former law student and is a fan of the works of Oscar Wilde?

19 Who are the two Sri Lankan batsmen to score Test match triple centuries?

20 Which side dismissed Sri Lanka for their lowest ever One Day International total of 55 in 1986?

Answers on page 214

West Indies

QUIZ 43

1 What colour do the West Indies usually wear in One Day Internationals?

2 Which batsman hit a 69 ball century in a Test match against Australia in 2004?

3 The West Indies enjoyed a run of 26 Test matches without defeat under the leadership of which captain?

4 Who took seven for 66 on his Test debut against England at Old Trafford in 2007?

5 Which unlikely opponents skittled the West Indies for just 25 in 1969?

6 Which West Indian great was born in Panama?

7 Which West Indian pair hold the record for the highest ever tenth wicket partnership in a One Day International?

8 Which opening batsman made 93 and 107 on his Test debut against India in 1974?

9 Which alliterative West Indian won a Man of the Match award against Zimbabwe in 2001, despite not batting and taking no wickets or catches?

10 West Indies bowled England out for what total in 1994: 36, 46 or 56?

11 England returned the compliment in 2004 bowling the West Indies out for what score: 37, 47 or 57?

Answers on page 214

12 Who are the four batsmen to score a Test match triple century for the West Indies?

13 Andy Roberts, Viv Richards and Curtly Ambrose are all from which island?

14 The West Indies beat England 5-0 in which two years of the 1980s?

15 Who is the only West Indian to score a century in his 100th Test match: Viv Richards, Gordon Greenidge or Brian Lara?

16 Which West Indian is the only man to carry his bat in three separate Test match innings?

17 Who smashed a century from just 71 balls against Australia at Perth in 1975/76: Roy Fredericks, Larry Gomes or Alvin Kallicharran?

18 True or false: Milton Small, who played two Test matches for the West Indies in 1984, is the brother of England seamer Gladstone Small?

19 Which West Indian is the only man in Test history to score a century in five consecutive Test match innings: Everton Weekes, Frank Worrell or Clyde Walcott?

20 In which West Indian capital would you find the Queen's Park Oval?

Answers on page 214

Zimbabwe

1 In what year did Zimbabwe make their Test debut: 1990, 1991 or 1992?

2 Who did they play in their first Test and what was the result?

3 What colour do Zimbabwe normally wear in One Day Internationals?

4 Zimbabwe shocked which country in the 1983 World Cup?

5 Who with an unbeaten 69 and four for 42, was named Man of the Match in that famous game?

6 Which 33-year-old chicken farmer took a hat-trick against England in a One Day International in 1997?

7 Zimbabwe won only one match in the 1992 Cricket World Cup. Who did they beat: England, Sri Lanka or Australia?

8 Which two brothers are Zimbabwe's two leading Test run scorers?

9 Which leg spinner has Zimbabwe's best Test bowling figures of eight for 109?

10 When asked by Glenn McGrath why he was so fat, which Zimbabwean replied 'because every time I make love to your wife she gives me a biscuit'?

Answers on page 214

11 Who was the first black player to play for Zimbabwe?

12 Zimbabwe gained their maiden Test match victory against which country?

13 True or false: Zimbabwe have never won a Test match against England?

14 Which Zimbabwe cricketer shares a name with a famous political adviser?

15 Who is Zimbabwe's most capped Test cricketer?

16 Zimbabwe beat which country in the 2007 World Twenty20?

17 Which Zimbabwe and Tasmania all rounder's first names are Arnoldus Mauritius?

18 Which Zimbabwean batsman, who later coached in English county cricket, scored 266 against Sri Lanka in 1994?

19 Which all rounder won three Man of the Match awards in the 1999 World Cup?

20 Which opening batsman scored a then World Record 380 against Zimbabwe in 2003?

Answers on page 214

Derbyshire CCC

1 What is the name of Derbyshire's principal ground: The County Ground, The Baseball Ground or The Circle?

2 Derbyshire's One Day side have what nickname?

3 Which Australian captained Derbyshire in 2007?

4 How many times have Derbyshire won the County Championship: never, once or twice?

5 Who is Derbyshire's all time leading First Class run scorer?

6 Derbyshire scored their highest ever County Championship total of 801 for 8 declared in 2007. Who were their opponents?

7 Which Irish pace bowler played for Derbyshire during the 2007 season?

8 Which Dane took 434 First Class wickets for Derbyshire between 1983 and 1994?

9 What is the name of Derbyshire's out ground at Chesterfield?

10 In what year did Derbyshire win their one and only Sunday League title: 1989, 1990 or 1991?

11 In what year did Derbyshire win the Benson and Hedges Cup?

Answers on page 214

12 Derbyshire's badge is made up of a crown and which type of flower?

13 True or false: Devon Malcolm once opened the batting for Derbyshire?

14 Which former Derbyshire wicketkeeper shares his name with a former West Brom striker and a Scottish dart player?

15 Who was the last English Derbyshire player to be named as one of Wisden's Five Cricketers of the Year?

16 True or false: Michael Holding played for Derbyshire?

17 Which current England selector started his First Class career at Derbyshire?

18 Which Derbyshire player was the passenger in David Gower's ill-fated Tiger Moth flight?

19 Which Derbyshire wicketkeeper was famous for his fidgeting behind the stumps?

20 Which former Indian captain played for Derbyshire between 1991 and 1994?

Answers on page 214

Durham CCC

QUIZ 46

1 What is the name of Durham's home ground?

2 In what year were Durham awarded First Class status: 1990, 1991 or 1992?

3 Who was the first Durham player to be capped by England?

4 Which Australian batsman was Durham's first overseas player in County Cricket?

5 Which Durham all rounder took all 10 wickets in an innings against Hampshire in 2007?

6 What is the nickname of Durham's One Day team: Ducks, Dragons or Dynamos?

7 In what year did Durham win their maiden First Class trophy?

8 England fielded three Durham players in a Test match in 2007. Who were the three players?

9 Which two Durham players would you find on a hot dog stand?

10 Durham's maiden First Class win came at which Football League ground?

11 Which England selector was Durham captain during their maiden First Class season?

12 Which of the following hasn't played for Durham: David Boon, Mike Hussey or Mark Waugh?

13 Durham's home ground is overlooked by which castle?

14 Who did Durham play in their first One Day final at Lord's?

15 Steve Harmison is a fan of which football club: Middlesbrough, Newcastle or Sunderland?

16 Durham's highest First Class total of 645 for 6 declared came against which county?

17 True or false: Durham have never been involved in a tied match?

18 Who is Durham's all time leading wicket taker with 518?

19 Which Australian scored Durham's highest individual score with 273 against Hampshire in 2002?

20 Durham's Paul Collingwood made his Test debut against which country?

Answers on page 215

QUIZ 47 Essex CCC

1 Essex play most of their home matches in which town: Chelmsford or Colchester?

2 What is the nickname of the Essex One Day side?

3 In what year did Essex win their first County Championship: 1978, 1979 or 1980?

4 True or false: Essex were the only side to bowl out Australia's 1948 'Invincibles' in a day?

5 Who is Essex's all time leading run scorer?

6 Which all rounder and later 'Test Match Special' commentator was Essex captain from 1961 to 1966?

7 Which former Essex and England batsman had the nickname Nashwan?

8 Essex dismissed which county for just 14 in 1983?

9 In what year did Essex win their first Sunday League crown?

10 Which Essex spinner made his Test debut in the same game as Shane Warne's Ashes debut?

11 Which Essex batsman scored 60 and 104 not out on his Test debut in 2006?

12 Three of what appear on the Essex badge: eagles, lions or swords?

Answers on page 215

13 Which player, whose surname also ends in i, replaced Ronnie Irani as Essex captain?

14 Who did Essex beat to win their first Benson and Hedges Cup trophy?

15 Which 1966 Football World Cup winner played First Class cricket for Essex?

16 Which Essex all rounder made his England One Day International debut against Australia in February 2007?

17 In the 1993 Ashes series four Essex players played in the same England XI. Can you name them?

18 True or false: Steve Waugh played County Cricket for Essex?

19 Which former Essex and England captain was known as The Gnome of Essex?

20 How many times did Essex win the County Championship between 1979 and 1992: four, five or six?

Glamorgan CCC

1 What is the name of Glamorgan's ground in Cardiff?

2 Which Glamorgan player was honoured as a Druid at the National Eisteddfod?

3 How many times have Glamorgan won the County Championship: once, twice or three times?

4 Glamorgan captain David Hemp played for which country in the 2007 World Cup?

5 Who with 34,056 runs, is Glamorgan's all time leading run scorer?

6 Which Glamorgan player was mentioned in a song by the Manic Street Preachers?

7 Which Glamorgan bowler made his Test debut against India in 2002?

8 Which diminutive former Glamorgan batsman shares a name with a former West Ham, Everton and England striker?

9 Who was Glamorgan captain during their 1997 County Championship winning season?

10 Two Glamorgan players played for England against West Indies in 1991. Can you name them?

11 Which Glamorgan batsman captained England on their 1972/73 tour to India?

12 True or false: Simon Jones was voted the 9th Sexiest Man in the World in a poll by *New Woman* magazine?

13 Who said 'playing for Glamorgan is like playing rugby for Wales. Playing for England is like playing for the British Lions'?

14 Who is Glamorgan's all time leading First Class wicket taker?

15 True or false: Glamorgan have never appeared at Lord's in a domestic One Day final?

16 Glamorgan play matches in which North Wales seaside town?

17 Which of the following hasn't played for Glamorgan: Ian Bishop, Hamish Anthony or Sir Viv Richards?

18 Glamorgan's highest individual score of 309 not out was made by which batsman in 2000?

19 Which unfortunate Glamorgan bowler was hit for six sixes by Sir Garfield Sobers in 1968?

20 What is the nickname of the Glamorgan One Day side?

Answers on page 215

Gloucestershire CCC

1 What is the nickname of the Gloucestershire's One Day team: Griffins, Gladiators or Golden Bears?

2 How many times have Gloucestershire been Champion County: once, twice or three times?

3 Which Gloucestershire seamer played his one and only Test match for England against Australia in 1997?

4 Who was Gloucestershire's first ever captain?

5 Who is Gloucesterhsire's all time leading run scorer?

6 How many One Day competitions did Gloucestershire win between 1999 and 2004: six, seven or eight?

7 True or false: Mike Proctor took two all LBW hat-tricks for Gloucestershire?

8 Which West Indian paceman played for Gloucestershire between 1984 and 1998?

9 What is wicketkeeper 'Jack' Russell's real first name?

10 Which Gloucestershire batsman had the nickname Steamy?

11 Which Gloucestershire paceman had the middle name Valentine?

12 Who did Gloucestershire beat in the 1999 Benson and Hedges Cup final?

Answers on page 215

13 Which Gloucestershire all rounder played 10 One Day Internationals for England between 1999 and 2000?

14 What do the initials W.G. of W.G. Grace stand for?

15 Which batsman scored Gloucestershire's all time highest individual score of 341 against Middlesex in 2004?

16 Which former Gloucestershire batsman holds the record for the most sixes in a First Class innings with 16?

17 Which Gloucestershire seamer is said to be 'never knowingly under-bowled'?

18 Gloucestershire's all time leading wicket taker shares a name with a famous jazz musician. Can you name him?

19 In what year were Gloucestershire last crowned Champion County: 1877, 1947 or 1977?

20 In what year did Gloucestershire complete a One Day treble of the Benson and Hedges Cup, Natwest Trophy and National League?

Answers on page 215

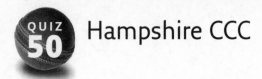

Hampshire CCC

1 What is the name of Hampshire's main home ground?

2 How many times have Hampshire won the County Championship: once, twice or three times?

3 Hampshire scored their highest ever total in a First Class match in 2005. Who were the opposition?

4 Which current Hampshire batsman shares a name with a former West Indies captain?

5 True or false: Hampshire were once bowled out for 15 in their first innings but still went on to win the match?

6 Which Hampshire and England player was known as The Judge?

7 Who captained Hampshire between 1985 and 1995?

8 Who did Hampshire beat in the final of the 2005 Friends Provident Trophy?

9 Which Hampshire bowler of the 1980s and 1990s has a first name that sounds like an article of clothing?

10 Which of the following Australians hasn't played County Cricket for Hampshire: Matthew Hayden, Shane Watson or Justin Langer?

11 What is Hampshire's One Day side known as: Hawks, Hounds or Hurricanes?

12 In what year did Hampshire last win the County Championship?

13 David Gower joined Hampshire from which county?

14 With 2,669 wickets, who is Hampshire's all time leading wicket taker?

15 Which Dutch player was Hampshire's leading wicket taker in 1989?

16 Which former Hampshire all rounder won three Man of the Match awards for Zimbabwe at the 1999 World Cup?

17 Which Hampshire batsman has the nickname Creepy?

18 Which legendary West Indian opened the batting for Hampshire in the 1970s and 1980s?

19 The father and grandfather of which current Hampshire bowler also played First Class cricket?

20 What two items feature on the Hampshire CCC badge?

Answers on page 215

Kent CCC

1   What is the nickname of the Kent One Day team?

2   What is the name of Kent's home ground in Canterbury?

3   In what year did Kent last win the County Championship: 1978, 1979 or 1980?

4   Which group of protesters burnt down the Kent pavilion in 1913?

5   Which current Kent player was born in Papua New Guinea?

6   Which Kent player was named a Wisden Cricketer of the Year in 1970?

7   Which Irish born seamer played three Test matches for England in the early 1990s?

8   True or false: Kent's Arthur Fagg is the only batsman to hit a double century in both innings of a First Class match?

9   Which spinner is the only player to play a Test match alongside Kent's Colin Cowdrey and his son Chris?

10   Which Kent bowler took 297 Test wickets for England?

11   Which current Kent player was born in Copenhagen, Denmark?

12   What colour is the horse on the Kent CCC badge?

13 Who is Kent's all time leading run scorer: Colin Cowdrey, Frank Woolley or Les Ames?

14 Who did Kent beat in the final of the 2007 Twenty20 Cup?

15 Which current international umpire captained Kent from 1991 to 1996?

16 Which former Kent captain has an Honours degree in Politics and International Relations?

17 Which of the following Sri Lankans hasn't been an overseas player for Kent: Aravinda de Silva, Lasith Malinga or Sanath Jayasuriya?

18 Which Kent spinner played two Test matches for England in 1996?

19 Which Kent bowler lists his favourite other sports as base jumping and snail racing?

20 In what year did Kent last win the One Day league?

Answers on page 215

Lancashire CCC

1   What is the nickname of Lancashire's One Day team:
Lions, Leopards or Lightning?

2   True or false: Lancashire's former captain Mark Chilton
was actually born in Yorkshire?

3   In what year did Lancashire last win the County
Championship outright: 1934, 1954 or 1974?

4   Which Lancashire wicketkeeper had the nickname
Chucky?

5   Which legendary West Indian batsman played for
Lancashire from 1968 to 1986?

6   The outfield at Old Trafford was damaged in 2007 after
a concert by which band?

7   Who won the Man of the Match award in a Lord's final
despite scoring a duck and not bowling?

8   Who scored 366 in a County Championship match in
1990?

9   One end of the ground at Old Trafford is named after
which legendary bowler?

10   True or false: Lancashire were runners-up in all four
competitions between 2004 and 2006?

11   Who smashed 24 runs in an over in near darkness to
win a 1971 Gillette Cup semi-final against
Gloucestershire?

12 Which bowler took six for 18 against Essex in the final of the 1996 Natwest Trophy?

13 Which former Lancashire player played against England for South Australia then went on to play for Italy?

14 Which Lancashire seam bowler is the only player to play for three counties in a single County Championship season?

15 Which current Lancashire player was named Virgin's Celebrity Dad of the Year 2007?

16 Which Everton and England footballer played under 19 cricket for Lancashire?

17 Which Lancashire opener also took 108 wickets with his occasional leg breaks?

18 Which Lancashire player is a cousin of boxer Amir Khan?

19 Which legendary 19th century Lancashire player shares a name with a long time Coronation Street actor?

20 Who is Lancashire's all time leading run scorer?

Answers on page 216

Leicestershire CCC

1 What is the name of Leicestershire's main home ground?

2 In what year did Leicestershire last win the County Championship: 1978, 1988 or 1998?

3 Leicesterhire played in the first ever Benson and Hedges Cup final. Who did they play in the final?

4 Which Leicestershire player played for England at the 2007 World Cup?

5 Who did Leicestershire face in the final of 2004 Twenty20 Cup?

6 What are Leicestershire's One Day team known as?

7 Which West Indian was named as one of Wisden's Five Cricketers of the Year while playing at Leicestershire in 1998?

8 Which England footballer also played second XI cricket with Leicestershire?

9 Two Leicestershire players were named in England's Twenty20 World Cup squad. Who were they?

10 Which stylish English left-hander played for Leicestershire between 1975 and 1989?

11 Which left arm seamer took 60 wickets to help Leicestershire to the County Championship in 1998?

Answers on page 216

12 Who beat Leicestershire in the final of the 1998 Benson and Hedges Cup?

13 Who is the odd man out: Devon Malcolm, Phil DeFreitas, Chris Lewis or Gladstone Small?

14 At which public school do Leicestershire sometimes play home matches?

15 Who was the captain when Leicestershire won the County Championship in 1975?

16 Which Leicestershire player was dubbed 'Lord Lucan' by the media due to his lack of appearances on England's tour to the West Indies in 1986?

17 Who played his one and only Test for England on the 1986/87 tour to Australia?

18 Who played a First Class match for Leicestershire then a football match for Doncaster Rovers on the same evening?

19 Leicestershire captain Hylton Ackerman is from which country?

20 In what decade did Leicestershire twice win the Sunday League?

Answers on page 216

QUIZ
54

Middlesex CCC

1   What is the nickname of the Middlesex One Day team?

2   Middlesex skipper Ed Smith wrote a book on which sport?

3   Middlesex conceded their highest ever score of 851 for seven in 2007. Who were their opponents?

4   Which two members of the 2007 Middlesex squad were born in Dublin?

5   What is the middle name of former Middlesex spinner Phil Edmonds: Harry, Herbert or Henri?

6   Which Middlesex batsman made his England Test debut in India in 2006?

7   Which of the following Australians hasn't played for Middlesex: Glen McGrath, Justin Langer, Stuart Clark or Jason Gillespie?

8   Who captained Middlesex to the County Championship in 1985, 1990 and 1993?

9   What colour shirts did Middlesex wear during their 2007 Twenty20 Cup campaign?

10   Which Middlesex player was the first black player to play Test cricket for England?

11   Dennis Compton played cricket for Middlesex and football for which club?

Answers on page 216

12 Whose career was ended after being hit in the eye by a bail?

13 What is former Middlesex captain Mike Brearley's profession?

14 There are three of what on the Middlesex badge?

15 Alan Richardson joined Middlesex from which county?

16 Which former Middlesex player is England's highest Test run scorer not to make a century?

17 Who did Middlesex beat by just two runs in the 1986 Benson and Hedges Cup final?

18 Who is Middlesex's all time leading First Class run scorer: Mike Gatting, Patsy Hendren or Andrew Strauss?

19 Who is Middlesex's all time leading First Class wicket taker?

20 Which West Indies and Middlesex paceman had the nickname Diamond?

Answers on page 216

Northamptonshire CCC

1 Where do Northamptonshire play their home games: Waddon Road, Wantage Road or Layer Road?

2 How many times have Northamptonshire won the County Championship: never, once or twice?

3 Which Northamptonshire batsman scored three centuries for England against the West Indies in 1984?

4 What is the nickname of the Northamptonshire One Day team?

5 Which Northamptonshire player won the BBC Sports Personality of the Year Award in 1975?

6 Which two Northamptonshire players played for England in the 1990 Test series against West Indies?

7 Who did Northamptonshire beat in the 1992 Natwest Trophy final?

8 Monty Panesar made his Test debut against which country?

9 Which Northamptonshire player was born in Dublin?

10 Which Australian recorded Northamptonshire's highest ever individual score against Somerset in 2003?

11 What heraldic emblem is on the Northamptonshire badge?

Answers on page 216

12 Which big hitting Northamptonshire opener had the nickname Ned?

13 Northamptonshire coach Kepler Wessels played Test cricket for which two countries?

14 Which portly player scored 0 and 210 not out on his county debut?

15 Who beat Northamptonshire in the 1990 Natwest Trophy final?

16 Which West Indian paceman took 318 wickets for Northamptonshire between 1989 and 1996?

17 Which Northamptonshire spinner has the middle name of Fred and the nickname of Cheese?

18 Who did Northamptonshire beat in the 1976 Natwest Trophy final?

19 Who is Northamptonshire's all time leading First Class run scorer?

20 Who did Northamptonshire beat by six runs in the 1980 Benson and Hedges Cup final?

Answers on page 216

Nottinghamshire CCC

QUIZ
56

1 Who was the Nottinghamshire captain in 2007?

2 What is the nickname of the Nottinghamshire One Day team?

3 Which West Indian all rounder was the last player to take 100 wickets and score 1,000 runs in a season?

4 Which Nottinghamshire bowler was at the centre of the Bodyline controversy?

5 Who did Nottinghamshire beat to win the 1987 Natwest Trophy?

6 Which Nottinghamshire wicketkeeper played 16 Tests for England in the late 1980s?

7 Nottinghamshire recorded their highest ever total of 791 in the County Championship in 2007. Who were their opponents?

8 Which Nottinghamshire pairing opened the batting for England against Pakistan in 1987?

9 Who captained Nottinghamshire to the County Championship in 1981?

10 Which current Nottinghamshire player has a name which sounds like an animated cartoon character?

11 Which Nottinghamshire and England batsman was named one of Wisden's Five Cricketers of the Year in 1980?

12 Who beat Nottinghamshire in the final of the 2006 Twenty20 Cup?

13 In what year did Nottinghamshire last win the County Championship?

14 Which New Zealander took 662 wickets for Nottinghamshire between 1978 and 1987?

15 How tall is Will Jefferson?

16 Who did Nottinghamshire beat to claim the 1989 Benson and Hedges Cup?

17 Who is Nottinghamshire's all time leading run scorer?

18 How many times have Nottinghamshire won the One Day league: once, twice or three times?

19 Which of the following New Zealanders hasn't played for Nottinghamshire: Chris Cairns, Dion Nash or Daniel Vettori?

20 Which former Nottinghamshire player was awarded a knighthood in 1975?

Answers on page 216

Somerset CCC

1   Who scored 322 for Somerset against Warwickshire in 1985?

2   Which Australian captained Somerset in 2007?

3   What is the nickname of Somerset's One Day side: Sharks, Sabres or Stallions?

4   How many times have Somerset won the County Championship: never, once or twice?

5   Who did Somerset beat to win the 2005 Twenty20 Cup final?

6   In what year did Ian Botham make his Somerset debut: 1974, 1975 or 1976?

7   True or false: former Somerset wicketkeeper Derek Taylor's full name is Derek John Somerset Taylor?

8   Three out of the Wisden's Five Cricketers of the Year in 1980 were Somerset players. Can you name them?

9   What was Andrew Caddick's job before becoming a full-time cricketer: plasterer and tiler, funeral director or golf course greenkeeper?

10   True or false: Somerset didn't win their first trophy until 1979?

11   Which Dutch seamer played for Somerset between 1990 and 1993?

12 Which Somerset batsman is known as Bangers due to his liking for sausages?

13 Who scored two centuries for Somerset in the 2006 Twenty20 Cup?

14 Which Somerset off spinner made his Test debut against Pakistan in 1982?

15 Which Australian didn't play for Somerset: Allan Border, Greg Chappell or Steve Waugh?

16 Which current Somerset player was born in Kuala Lumpur, Malaysia?

17 Somerset beat which county in the 2001 Cheltenham & Gloucester Trophy final?

18 What appears on the Somerset county badge?

19 Which fortysomething Yorkshireman captained Somerset in the 1970s?

20 Which Somerset player made his one and only Test appearance against India in 2006?

Answers on page 216

QUIZ 58 Surrey CCC

1 Surrey changed the name of their One Day team from Lions to what in 2006?

2 Which Surrey player has scored two One Day double hundreds?

3 True or false: The Oval used to be a market garden?

4 Which Surrey player partnered Sarah Brightman on the BBC singing show *Just The Two Of Us*?

5 Who is Surrey's most capped England player?

6 Who is the all time leading run scorer for Surrey?

7 Surrey scored a World Record total for a 50 over match against Gloucestershire in 2007. How many did they score: 476, 486 or 496?

8 Who did Surrey beat in the final of the 2003 Twenty20 Cup?

9 Which Cornishman kept wicket for Surrey and England in the 1980s?

10 For how many consecutive seasons did Surrey win the County Championship in the 1950s?

11 Who led Surrey to County Championship victory in 1999, 2000 and 2002?

12 Which Surrey seamer after winning his first Test cap in 1993 had to wait until 2003 to win his second?

13 Which Surrey bowler who took 1,924 First Class wickets was awarded a knighthood in 1996?

14 Which Surrey and West Indies paceman who terrorised batsmen in the 1980s, had the middle name Theophilus?

15 In what year did Surrey win the Natwest Trophy: 1982, 1986 or 1990?

16 Mark Ramprakash joined Surrey from which county?

17 The highest score conceded by Surrey in an innings was 863 in 1990. Which county scored them?

18 Which of the following hasn't been played at The Oval: Baseball, American Football or Lacrosse?

19 Which former prime minister was President of Surrey in 2000 and 2001?

20 Which former Surrey player shares a name with a Roman Emperor?

Answers on page 217

Sussex CCC

1 What is the nickname of the Sussex One Day team?

2 In what year did Sussex win their first County Championship: 1983, 1993 or 2003?

3 Sussex won the County Championship and the Cheltenham & Gloucester Trophy in 2006. Who were the runners-up in both competitions?

4 Which Zimbabwean holds the record for the highest individual score made by a Sussex player?

5 The Sussex crest depicts six of what mythological bird?

6 Which former Sussex player also held the long jump World Record and was offered the throne of Albania?

7 Which former Sussex and England player was born in Milan?

8 All rounder Luke Wright began his career at which county?

9 True or false: former Sussex captain John Barclay was born in France?

10 Which Sussex spinner was the first bowler this century to take 100 First Class wickets?

11 In what year did Sussex win their one and only John Player League title?

12 Who replaced Peter Moores as Sussex coach after Moores took the England job?

13 Which former Sussex and England captain was born in Queenstown, South Africa?

14 Which Sussex pace bowler took 202 Test wickets for England at 26.66?

15 Sussex wicketkeeper Matt Prior made his Test debut against which side?

16 Which Sussex bowler had to remodel his action after being suspected of throwing?

17 Three Pakistan internationals played for Sussex in 2007. Can you name them?

18 Who did Sussex beat in the final of the 1986 Natwest Trophy?

19 Who beat Sussex in the final of the 1993 Natwest Trophy?

20 Which member of the Sussex team is also known as Grizzly?

Answers on page 217

QUIZ 60 Warwickshire CCC

1 Where do Warwickshire play their home games?

2 Warwickshire won three trophies in the same season in what year?

3 What was the only trophy they missed out on that year?

4 Who is Warwickshire's all time leading run scorer?

5 Warwickshire's all time leading wicket taker gives his name to a stand at their home ground. What is his name?

6 Who hit the winning runs in Warwickshire's epic win over Sussex in the 1993 Natwest Trophy final?

7 Which Warwickshire captain was born in Kowloon, Hong Kong?

8 Who beat Warwickshire in the final of the 2005 Cheltenham & Gloucester Trophy?

9 Who is the only Warwickshire player to score 10,000 runs and take 1,000 wickets?

10 Which West Indian batsman scored 11,615 First Class runs for Warwickshire between 1968 and 1977?

11 What is the nickname of Warwickshire's One Day team: The Warriors, The Bears or The Werewolves?

12 Which wicketkeeper holds the record for the most sixes in an innings by a Warwickshire player in a First Class match?

Answers on page 217

13 Which Warwickshire seamer took the winning catch to seal England's victory in the 1986/87 Ashes series?

14 Who did Warwickshire beat in the final of the 1989 Natwest Trophy?

15 True or false: comedian Frank Skinner is a Warwickshire fan?

16 Who took 757 First Class wickets but played only two Test matches for England?

17 Warwickshire keeper Tim Ambrose was born in which country?

18 Which Warwickshire all rounder played football at Hampden Park for Scotland under 18s?

19 Who captained Warwickshire to the 2004 County Championship title?

20 Which Warwickshire and England captain also represented England at Rugby Union?

Answers on page 217

Worcestershire CCC

QUIZ 61

1 Who scored Worcestershire's highest individual First Class score of 405 not out against Somerset in 1988?

2 Which Worcestershire spinner in 1995 took a wicket with his first ball in Test cricket?

3 Which Worcestershire seamer was the leading First Class wicket taker in 1985 and 1987?

4 Who was Worcestershire captain in 2007?

5 Who did Worcestershire beat in the final of the 1991 Benson and Hedges Cup?

6 Former captain Phil Neale played football for which two Lincolnshire clubs?

7 Which New Zealander played for Worcestershire between 1967 and 1982?

8 Worcestershire won the County Championship twice in the 1980s. What were the years?

9 Which Worcestershire bowler took five wickets in his debut Test match against South Africa in 2003?

10 How many Test matches did Steve Rhodes play for England: 1, 11 or 21?

11 True or false: Graeme Hick has scored a century of centuries?

12 What fruit appears on the Worcestershire CCC crest?

13 Which Australian captained Worcestershire from 1995 to 1999?

14 Which Worcestershire opener played five Tests for England in 1988 and 1989?

15 Who did Worcestershire beat in the final of the 1994 Natwest Trophy?

16 Which all rounder hasn't played for Worcestershire: Ian Botham, Kapil Dev, Imran Khan or Richard Hadlee?

17 Which current First Class umpire was part of the Worcestershire championship winning side of 1974: Vanburn Holder or John Holder?

18 Which seam bowler is Worcestershire's all time leading One Day wicket taker?

19 Who is Worcestershire's all time leading run scorer?

20 How many times did Worcestershire win the Sunday League: two, three or four?

Answers on page 217

Yorkshire CCC

QUIZ 62

1 What is the name of the Yorkshire One Day team: Phoenix, Flat Caps or Tykes?

2 Who was Yorkshire's captain in 2007?

3 Who captained Yorkshire to the County Championship title in 2001?

4 Which chat show host had trials for Yorkshire: Richard Whiteley, Russell Harty or Michael Parkinson?

5 Who was the first overseas player to play for Yorkshire?

6 Who is Yorkshire's all time leading First Class run scorer?

7 True or false: Yorkshire's Michael Vaughan was actually born in Lancashire?

8 Who is the only Yorkshire player to score a century and a double century in the same match?

9 Which Australian hasn't played for Yorkshire: Greg Blewett, Darren Lehmann or Damien Fleming?

10 Who did Yorkshire beat in the final of the 2002 Cheltenham & Gloucester Trophy?

11 In what year did Yorkshire win their only Sunday League title: 1973, 1983 or 1993?

12 Three Yorkshire players have captained England but not Yorkshire. Stanley Jackson is one, can you name the other two?

13 Who was the first Yorkshire-born Asian to play for the club?

14 Which Yorkshire player hit 50 off only 14 balls in a Twenty20 Cup match in 2006?

15 True or false: Ray Illingworth captained Yorkshire at the age of 50?

16 Which young spinner took six for 67 on his Championship debut against Warwickshire in 2006?

17 Which legendary Yorkshire and England bowler had the middle name Sewards?

18 Who is Yorkshire's all time leading wicket taker?

19 True or false: Yorkshire's Arnie Sidebottom played professional football for Manchester City?

20 Which Yorkshireman played 10 Test matches for England in the 1980s and had a top score of 99?

Answers on page 217

Anagrams

Find the player from the following anagrams.

1 Be Letter

2 Amnesty Apron

3 Envies Knee Trip

4 Earn Ash New

5 A Mailman Trait Huh

6 Tricking Pony

7 Callow Duo Loping

8 Enchilada Trunks

9 He Cheddar Liar

10 I Am Bath No

11 Paved Ilk

12 Hazer Ah Ken

13 Unsavory Gulag

14 Trouser Cymbal

15 Caveman Hail Ugh

16 Titan Evildoer

17 Grim Salad Itch

18 Alcohol Punks

19 Parka Harms Mark

20 Haiku Sonny

Answers on page 217

Bad Boys

QUIZ 64

1 Which England captain was fined £1,000 after being spotted in a lap dancing club the night before a match?

2 Which two Australians bet on their team losing at odds of 500/1 in the 1981 Ashes Test at Headingley?

3 Which England all rounder was banned in 1986 after admitting to smoking cannabis?

4 Which former Indian captain was banned for life after being implicated in a match fixing scandal?

5 Which England player was fined £2,000 for the so called 'dirt in the pocket' affair in 1994?

6 Javed Miandad was involved in an on-field spat with which Indian wicketkeeper at the 1992 World Cup?

7 Which Warwickshire wicketkeeper tested positive for taking cannabis?

8 Which West Indian fast bowler kicked over the stumps after having a caught behind appeal turned down in New Zealand in 1980?

9 True or false: Shane Warne was banned for taking a weight loss drug?

10 England players were rebuked for leaving what on the wicket against India in 2007: jelly beans, fruit pastilles or wine gums?

Answers on page 218

11 Which South African admitted match fixing and was banned from cricket for life in 2000?

12 Which England captain was involved in an infamous dispute with Pakistani umpire Shakoor Rana in 1987?

13 Which Indian was fined 50 per cent of his match fee after being found guilty of applying sugar-coated saliva to the ball during a One Day International against Zimbabwe?

14 Which West Indian was charged with stabbing his cousin in January 2004?

15 Which big hitting former England batsman pleaded guilty to a charge of deception over a mortgage scam in 2007?

16 Which Australian arrived at the ground drunk before a game with Bangladesh in 2005 and subsequently received a two game ban?

17 Which former Warwickshire all rounder, who was banned for using cocaine, now promotes cricket in inner city Los Angeles?

18 Which Australian leg spinner served a prison sentence for embezzlement?

19 Which batsman turned ICC match referee smashed his stumps after being bowled against Australia in 1988?

20 Which two England batsmen were fined for flying a Tiger Moth plane over the ground during a match between Queensland and England in 1991?

Answers on page 218

Beards and Moustaches

1 Which England player won the 2006 Beard of the Year award?

2 Which Australian all rounder and Sri Lankan bowler shared the Beard Liberation Front Beard of the World Cup 2007 award?

3 Which England captain was dubbed 'The Ayatollah' by the Australian media in 1979 due to his bushy beard?

4 England's players grew moustaches on their tour of Pakistan in 2005. Which spinner's effort made him look 'a bit like Hitler'?

5 Which moustachioed England swinger bowled England to victory in the Ashes Test at Edgbaston in 1985?

6 Who in 1986 went to the traditional England tour Christmas fancy dress party dressed as Diana Ross but drew the line at shaving off his moustache?

7 Who won back-to-back Beard of the Year awards in 2004 and 2005?

8 Which bearded wonder took 90 First Class wickets for Sussex in 2007?

9 Which moustachioed Australian made his Test debut against India in 1984 and took a total of 212 Test wickets?

10 Who is famous for his huge beard and was the first player of Asian origin to play Test cricket for South Africa?

11 The famously hirsute W. G. Grace played for which English county: Gloucestershire, Lancashire or Yorkshire?

12 Which moustachioed Tasmanian played 102 Test matches for Australia and also captained Durham between 1997 and 1999?

13 Which bearded Englishman played 35 Tests then went on to coach Ireland between 1995 and 2000?

14 Which Guyanese left-hander sported an impressive moustache during the majority of his 110 matches?

15 Which bearded Pakistani played 55 Test matches between 1990 and 2001, and holds the record for the highest One Day International score?

16 Which eccentric wicketkeeper was noted for his battered white hat, fantastic glove work and ever present moustache?

17 Which moustachioed England batsman smashed 18 runs off which moustachioed Australian bowler to claim an unlikely victory in Sydney in 1986?

18 Which Chappell brother regularly sported a full beard?

19 Which moustachioed New Zealander ran out Derek Randall while backing up in a Test match in 1977/78?

20 In 1990 which bushy 'tached opener scored the winning runs in England's first Test victory over the West Indies for 16 years?

Answers on page 218

Debuts

1 Which England left-hander scored a century at Lord's in his first Test innings in 2004 and was well on his way to another in the second innings before being run out by his captain?

2 Which all time great took just one wicket for 150 runs on his Test debut against India in 1992?

3 How old was Sachin Tendulkar when he made his Test match debut: 16, 17 or 18?

4 Which West Indian is the only player to score a century and a double century on his Test debut: Viv Richards, Rohan Kanhai or Lawrence Rowe?

5 How many runs did Graham Gooch score in the two innings of his Test debut: 0, 50 or 100?

6 Which Indian spinner took 16 wickets for 136 runs on his Test debut against the West Indies in 1988?

7 Which England seamer took seven for 43 at Lord's on his Test debut against the West Indies in 1995?

8 In 2001 which Bangladeshi debutant became the youngest player to score a Test century?

9 Which Indian is the only player to score centuries on debut in the Ranji, Duleep and Irani Trophy?

10 Which Scottish all rounder bagged a pair and took no wickets in his one and only Test appearance?

11 Ian Botham took five for 74 on his Test debut against which country?

12 Who is the youngest player to make his debut for England: Brian Close, Alastair Cook or Ian Botham?

13 What do Wasim Akram, Len Hutton, Michael Atherton and Larry Gomes all have in common?

14 Who took seven for 124 and scored 205 on his First Class debut and was the last white player to play for the West Indies?

15 Which stylish Indian batsman scored a century on his Test debut, then followed it up with two more centuries in the next two Test matches?

16 Sourav Ganguly scored a century on his Test debut against which country?

17 Which Australian seamer turned commentator took a hat-trick on his Test debut against Pakistan in 1994?

18 Which wicketkeeper captained New Zealand on his Test debut in India in 1995?

19 Which Sri Lankan wicketkeeper scored an unbeaten 201 on his Test debut against New Zealand in 1987?

20 Which South Africa and Yorkshire batsman scored 222 not out on his Test debut in 2002?

Answers on page 218

Family Affairs

1 Which pair of brothers made their Test debut against Australia at Trent Bridge in 1997?

2 True or false: Shaun Pollock is the son of former South African batsman Graeme Pollock?

3 Who were the first twins to play Test cricket?

4 In 1999 the Surrey playing staff contained three sets of brothers. Can you name them?

5 Zimbabwe's Ray Price is related to which famous golfer?

6 Ryan Sidebottom's father played one Test for England in 1985. What is his name?

7 Brothers Jeff and Martin Crowe are related to which Hollywood star?

8 Which two brothers played for Ireland in the 2007 World Cup?

9 Which two brothers made their ODI debuts in the same match but for different countries?

10 The son of which former England opening batsman made his international debut in 2007?

11 Which family has provided three generations of Test players, the first two for the West Indies, the third for England?

12 Fidel Edwards is the half-brother of which West Indian left arm bowler?

13 Richie Benaud's brother made his Test debut 20 years after Richie. What is his name?

14 Which Australian instructed his brother to bowl the last ball of a One Day International underarm to stop the opposition from hitting a six?

15 The father of which member of England's 2005 Ashes winning team played 15 Tests for England in the 1960s?

16 Which pair of brothers both took four for 53 on their England Test debut?

17 The father of which Gloucestershire seamer played 108 Test matches for the West Indies?

18 The grandsons of which two legendary England batsmen played for Middlesex in 2007?

19 Which pair of English brothers both umpired Test matches in the 1990s?

20 The father of England's most capped player also played eight Test matches for England. What are their names?

Answers on page 218

Golden Grahams

1   Which Graeme scored an unbeaten 405 against Somerset in 1988?

2   Which Graham is England's all time leading Test run scorer?

3   Graham Onions plays for which English county?

4   Which all rounder played 251 First Class matches for Somerset between 1985 and 2002, scoring over 8,000 runs and taking 604 wickets?

5   Graham Thorpe scored his highest Test score of 200 not out against which country?

6   Which Australian Graeme scored nine Test centuries between 1978 and 1988?

7   Graeme Welch captained which English county in 2007?

8   Who made his One Day International debut for England in 2000, then had to wait seven years to make his next appearance?

9   Who wrote an award winning diary of a season called *Fox on the Run*?

10   Who became South African captain in 2003 aged just 22?

11   Which Graham took 138 Test wickets for England between 1979 and 1989?

12 Graham Roope played for which English county?

13 True or false: Lancashire batsman Graham Lloyd is the son of Clive Lloyd?

14 Which Graham captained Australia to a 5–1 defeat in the 1977/78 Ashes series?

15 The brother and father of which Graham both captained England?

16 Which Graham played his two Test matches for England in 1981 and 1982?

17 Which all rounder now at Derbyshire was banned from the game for a year after testing positive for cocaine?

18 Graeme Pollock scored his highest Test score of 274 against which country: Australia, England or New Zealand?

19 How old was Graham Gooch when he retired from Test cricket: 39, 40 or 41?

20 Only one Sri Lankan called Graeme has played Test cricket. What is his surname?

Answers on page 218

Injuries

1 Glen McGrath missed the Ashes Test at Edgbaston in 2005 after treading on what: a cricket ball, a rugby ball or a stray dog?

2 Jason Gillespie broke his leg after a collision in the outfield with which Australian colleague?

3 Which England captain was known as 'poppadom fingers' due to the regularity with which he broke them?

4 Which Australian bowler dislocated a shoulder, rugby tackling a streaker in Perth in 1981?

5 Andy Lloyd's Test career lasted less than an hour after he was struck by a bouncer from which West Indian bowler?

6 Which former England captain broke his leg after being run over by his own car?

7 Which former England all rounder broke his ankle trying to break into his own house after snapping his front door key in the lock?

8 New Zealand opener Trevor Franklin suffered multiple leg fractures after being hit by what vehicle: golf buggy, car or an airport motorised luggage trolley?

9 Which West Indian helped Larry Gomes to a century batting one handed against England in 1984?

10 Which England fast bowler's knee shattered in Wellington, New Zealand in 1992?

11 Which England captain, after being hit by a Malcolm Marshall bouncer and sporting two black eyes, was famously asked, 'Where exactly did it hit you?'

12 Which all rounder got sunstroke after shaving his head on England's tour of the West Indies in 1994?

13 Simon Jones severely damaged his knee at which Australian ground?

14 Which opener scored a century on his Test debut after being called into the team after a late injury to Michael Vaughan?

15 Which Australian batted with a broken jaw in the Centenary Test?

16 Which Indian spinner bowled 14 overs against West Indies in 2002 despite having a broken jaw?

17 Graham Gooch had his finger broken by which West Indian bowler on England's 1990 tour of the Caribbean?

18 Which England all rounder injured his back after a chair collapsed while he was writing a letter?

19 Which giant opening batsman damaged tendons while trying to open his bathroom window?

20 True or false: Don Topley damaged his hand on a spring loaded letterbox while delivering a letter?

Answers on page 219

Name Game

1 Glen McGrath has which bird-related nickname?

2 Which West Indian batsman was known as The Master Blaster?

3 Which legendary West Indian openers real first name is Cuthbert?

4 The King of Spain was a moniker given to which England spinner?

5 Which current Australian seamer has the middle name Rupert?

6 Which Australian batsman was known as Tugga?

7 Which former Australian fast bowler, optometrist and now coach has the nickname Henry?

8 Which Middlesex bowler shares a name with a former member of pop group Take That?

9 Spinner Eddie Hemmings shares a name with a commentator on which sport: rugby union, rugby league or darts?

10 Skid is the nickname of which spinner turned broadcaster?

11 Punter is the nickname of which current Australian star?

12 What name was given to the Australian team which toured England in 1948?

13 Which English county captain shares a name with a professional wrestler: Chris Adams, Mark Chilton or Darren Gough?

14 Which member of England's 1986/87 Ashes winning team has the middle name Cleophas?

15 Which Sri Lankan seamer has the first names Warnakulasuriya Patabendige Ushantha Joseph?

16 What was Alec Stewart's nickname: The Boss, The Gaffer or The Chief?

17 Michael Vaughan's nickname of Virgil comes from which TV puppet show?

18 Bob Willis adopted his second middle name in honour of which singer?

19 What is Clive Lloyd's middle name: Herbert, Hubert or Schubert?

20 Which West Indian paceman was named after a former American President?

Answers on page 219

One Test Wonders

1   Which Glamorgan batsman made his one and only appearance against the Rest of the World in 1970?

2   Which St Kitts born seamer took 4-42 on his one and only Test appearance for England?

3   Which current international umpire played one Test for England against India in 1986?

4   Which Scottish all rounder played his sole Test on England's 1999 tour to South Africa?

5   Which Australian scored an unbeaten 54 in his only Test innings?

6   Which Durham spinner played one Test for West Indies against India in 2002?

7   Kabir Ali won his only Test cap against which country?

8   Whose Test career lasted just 33 minutes after being struck by a Malcolm Marshall bouncer?

9   Which Australian one Test wonder was also a professional Aussie Rules footballer?

10   Which Australia, Northants and Surrey quick bowler won his only Test cap against England in 1998?

11   Which player, who shares a name with a former England footballer, won his only cap against Australia in 1981?

12 Whose short Test career is best remembered for Graham Thorpe dropping a catch off his bowling?

13 Which Durham left-armer played one Test in England's 1996 series against Pakistan?

14 Sussex batsman Alan Wells won his only Test cap against which team in 1995?

15 Which St Vincent born seamer played for England against India in 1990?

16 Which West Indian scored 112 in his only Test innings in 1948?

17 Which New Zealander scored 107 and 56 in his only Test appearance?

18 In 1979 an Englishman played his only Test. Eighteen years later his son made his Test debut. Who is he?

19 Who had to cancel his wedding to make his only Test appearance for England in New Zealand in 1984?

20 The father of which current England seamer played one Test for England against Australia in 1985?

Answers on page 219

Portly Players

1 A fan smuggled a pig into the Gabba in 1982. The names of which two England players were written on the side of the porker?

2 Which solidly built Englishman was the first man to hit four sixes in an over in a One Day International?

3 Which Lancashire and England all rounder had the nicknames Bully and Oscar?

4 Which chunky Warwickshire opener later went on to coach Griqualand, Kenya, Scotland and Northern Districts?

5 Which stocky Indian spinner took six wickets in the One Day series between England and India in 2007?

6 Which portly Northamptonshire batsman has made seven First Class double centuries but has never played for England?

7 Who said 'Not bad for a fat lad' after being named Man of the Match in a One Day International in 2000?

8 Which sturdy English batsman made 221 against the West Indies in 2004?

9 Who confronted a spectator after repeatedly being called 'mota aaloo' (big potato)?

10 Who was banned from cricket for a year in 2003 after taking a banned weight loss pill?

11 Which England batsman was nicknamed Ollie due to his supposed likeness to rotund comedian Oliver Hardy?

12 Which Australian captain had the nickname Tubs?

13 Which Lancashire off spinner was famed for his almost endless capacity for fish and chip suppers?

14 Which chunky Australian allegedly drank 52 cans of lager on a flight from Sydney to London?

15 Who captained Sri Lanka to victory in the 1996 World Cup?

16 After Mark Waugh questioned his Test match credentials, which tubby England seamer is said to have replied 'at least I'm the best player in my family'?

17 Which infamously large goalkeeper from the 1900s also played four First Class matches for Derbyshire?

18 Which Australian was said to be too fat to play for his state side and was threatened with the loss of his South Australia contract if he didn't lose weight?

19 Which beefy batsman who played 30 Tests for Australia in the 1980s, was known as Fat Cat?

20 Former Australian skipper Warwick Armstrong was known as: The Big Unit, The Big Tank or The Big Ship?

Answers on page 219

Quotes

1 'If this bloke's a Test match bowler, then my backside is a fire engine'. Which player was David Lloyd describing when he first saw him bowl?

2 'You can't bring it back ... it's gone. I'll just spend the next 20 years worrying about it.' Who said it and what was he talking about?

3 Which unlikely Irishman outed himself as a cricket fan revealing 'There are many closet cricket fans among the nationalist community.'?

4 Which England batsman was 'more nervous than when I go out to bat for England' when he played darts against Women's World Champion Trina Gulliver?

5 Who revealed that his mum and grandma are always telling him 'Don't cut your hair': Ryan Sidebottom, Nathan Bracken or Lasith Malinga?

6 Which American actor and comedian described cricket as 'basically baseball on valium'?

7 Which Nobel Prize winning playwright said 'I tend to think that cricket is the greatest thing that God ever created on earth – certainly greater than sex, although sex isn't too bad either.'?

8 'Murali will complete 1,000 Test wickets but they would count as mere run-outs in my eyes.' Which former Indian spinner isn't impressed at the Sri Lankan's achievements?

9 Which England captain said he wanted to make the West Indies 'grovel'?

10 'If my mum was alive she could captain England to play West Indies ... hopeless, aren't they?' Who was giving his typically forthright opinion?

11 According to Colin Croft, which England batsman 'was sacrificed in the first Test ... he was set up to fail because they knew someone had to be dropped for Michael Vaughan. It was political.'?

12 What did Mark Lawrenson describe as 'being a great advert for cricket'?

13 Which umpire said 'Life without sport is like life without underpants.'?

14 Which England all rounder described himself as 'the fattest 20 year old in England'?

15 'I can drive a flock of sheep through the town centre, drink for free in no less than 64 pubs, and get a lift home with a policeman when I become inebriated. What more could you want?' Which all rounder was delighted after being made a freeman of his home town.

16 'If it had been a cheese roll, it would never have got past him', which batsman was Graham Gooch describing after he was bowled by Shane Warne?

17 Which former Australian seamer said 'I definitely believe if any of our batsmen get out to Ashley Giles in the Tests they should go out and hang themselves. But I am confident that won't happen.'?

18 Which Australian quickie said 'I enjoy hitting a batsman more than getting him out. I like to see blood on the pitch.'?

19 'When I go past a school and see children playing I often wish I had grown up here and got the chance to learn how to play'. Which Manchester based German footballer wishes he could play cricket?

20 'He's like Godfrey Evans behind there.' Which unlikely wicketkeeper was David Lloyd describing during the 2007 World Twenty20?

Answers on page 219

QUIZ 74 All Rounders

1 Which all rounder is England's leading Test wicket taker?

2 Who are the two men who have scored 8,000 Test runs and taken 200 Test wickets?

3 Which two players have scored a century and taken 10 wickets in the same Test match?

4 Who has taken more Test wickets: Kapil Dev or Richard Hadlee?

5 Imran Khan played domestic cricket for which two English counties?

6 Which oft injured Australian all rounder made his Test debut against Pakistan in 2005?

7 Which Lancastrian born all rounder co-hosts a radio breakfast show on Talk Sport?

8 Which New Zealand all rounder hit 87 sixes in his Test career?

9 Who is the only man to take six wickets and score a century in a One Day International?

10 Which Australian in 1963 became the first player to score 2,000 Test runs and take 200 Test wickets?

11 Which West Indian has the highest bowling average of anyone who has taken at least one hundred Test wickets?

12 Who took more Test wickets: Ian Botham or Imran Khan?

13 Who won 60 caps for the New Zealand All Blacks at rugby union and six One Day International caps for the New Zealand cricket team?

14 Which current Surrey all rounder played two Tests for England against Bangladesh in 2003?

15 Who is the only man to play in a County Championship and FA Cup winning side in the same year?

16 Which South African born all rounder captained England in the 1970s?

17 Which Pakistani is the only man to score 1,000 Test match runs without a 50?

18 Which two father and son combinations have all taken one hundred Test wickets?

19 Which South African all rounder took four wickets in four balls on his English county debut?

20 Which Scotland goalkeeper also played four games for the Scotland cricket team?

Answers on page 219

Big Hitters

1 Four men have hit six sixes in an over. Can you name them?

2 Which Australian holds the record for the most sixes hit in a single innings?

3 Which England all rounder hit five consecutive sixes at the end of a One Day International against India in 2007?

4 Who holds the record for the fastest Test match century?

5 Which West Indian smashed 117 from just 57 balls in the opening game of the World Twenty20?

6 Which Pakistani hit the fastest One Day International century against Sri Lanka in 1996?

7 Who scored England's fastest One Day International century against South Africa in 2005?

8 Adam Gilchrist hit a century against England in 2006 off how many deliveries: 56, 57 or 58?

9 Which Bangladeshi smashed a half century from just 26 balls against India in 2007?

10 Who holds the record for the most sixes hit in an English First Class season?

11 Shahid Afridi smashed 27 from an over bowled by which Indian spinner in a Test match in 2006?

12 Which New Zealander hit 87 sixes in just 62 Test matches?

13 Who is England's all time leading six hitter in Test cricket?

14 Which left-hander holds the record for the most sixes hit in a Test match innings?

15 Which Surrey batsman smashed 268 in a One Day game against Glamorgan in 2002?

16 Which Sri Lankan has hit the most sixes in the history of One Day International cricket?

17 What is the highest ever individual score in a One Day International: 188, 189 or 194?

18 Which Australian smashed 141 not out from just 70 balls for Somerset in a Twenty20 Cup match in 2006 but still ended up on the losing side?

19 Who was the first player to score a century in international Twenty20 cricket?

20 Which batsman hit more than 50 sixes in 1933, 1936 and 1938?

Answers on page 220

Captains

1   Who holds the record for the most Test wins as captain?

2   Who holds the record for the most Test defeats as captain?

3   Who captained England in the 2007 World Twenty20?

4   In what year did England field four captains in a single series against the West Indies?

5   Who were the four captains?

6   Who captained the ICC World Test XI against Australia in 2005?

7   Whose one and only Test match as England captain ended in a draw against New Zealand in 1999?

8   Who captained England in three Test matches in 1990, losing each one?

9   Who has captained England in the most Test matches?

10   Who led Pakistan for 17 Test matches yet wasn't involved in a single draw?

11   Which West Indies captain won the toss almost 70 per cent of the time in his 39 games in charge?

12   How many Test matches did England win under Mike Gatting's leadership: 2, 6 or 10?

13 Which Australian holds the record for the most consecutive Tests as captain?

14 What do Mark Taylor, Rashid Latif and Habibul Bashar have in common?

15 Who captained South Africa on their reintroduction to international cricket in 1992?

16 Which two skippers hold the record for the most Tests as captain without a win?

17 Who did Viv Richards replace as West Indies captain?

18 Who played the most Test matches before taking over the reins as captain?

19 Who holds the record for the most Test victories by an Indian captain?

20 Which England batsman averaged 58.72 when captain compared to just 35.93 when he wasn't in charge?

Answers on page 220

In the Field

1 Which England slip fielder took a stunning one handed catch to dismiss Adam Gilchrist in the 2005 Ashes series?

2 What is the record for the most catches taken by a non-wicketkeeper in a Test match innings: four, five or six?

3 Two Englishmen have taken 120 catches in Test matches. Colin Cowdrey is one who is the other?

4 Which South African famously dropped Steve Waugh in the 1999 World Cup?

5 Graham Gooch was dropped on 36 by which Indian at Lord's in 1990 on his way to a mammoth triple century?

6 Which West Indian ran out three Australian batsmen in the final of the 1975 World Cup?

7 What is the record for the most catches taken by a substitute in a Test innings: two, three or four?

8 Who has been run out the most times in Test cricket: Allan Border, Inzamam-ul-Haq or Carl Hooper?

9 The record for the most run outs in a Test match innings is: three, four or five?

10 Who dropped Kevin Pietersen on 15 while he was on his way to 158 against Australia at The Oval in 2005?

11 Out of 198 Test innings how many times was Inzamam-ul-Haq run out: six, seven or eight?

12 Which legendary South African fielder also represented his country at hockey?

13 Which West Indian spinner famously ran out Graham Gooch in MCC versus the Rest of the World at Lord's in 1987?

14 Which two South African batsmen were involved in a last wicket run out in the semi-final of the 1999 World Cup against Australia?

15 Substitute fielder Gary Pratt famously ran out which Australian batsman in the 2005 Ashes?

16 Which Indian holds the record for the most catches taken by a non-wicketkeeper in One Day Internationals?

17 What is the record for the most catches taken by a single fielder in a One Day International: four, five or six?

18 What was unusual about the dismissal of Wayne Phillips in the 1985 Ashes match at Edgbaston?

19 Which Australian took 51 catches off Shane Warne's bowling: Mark Taylor, Mark Waugh or Steve Waugh?

20 Lancashire's Neil Fairbrother was named after which great Australian fielder?

Answers on page 220

Left Arm Seamers

1 Only two left arm seamers have taken 300 Test wickets. Who are they?

2 Which left arm seamer was Man of the Series in the 2007 Test matches between England and India?

3 Which two Australian left arm seamers played in the 2007 World Cup?

4 Which New Zealand left-armer was the leading wicket taker in the 1999 World Cup?

5 Which England left-armer took 54 Test wickets between 1996 and 2001?

6 Which Indian was the first man to take a hat-trick in the first over of a Test match?

7 Who is the only seamer to take over 500 ODI wickets?

8 Which English left arm seamer took seven for 46 on his Test debut in India in 1976?

9 Which Australian took 186 Test wickets for Australia between 1953 and 1963?

10 The best bowling figures in a One Day International of eight for 19 were taken by which left arm seamer?

11 Murphy Su'a played 13 Tests for which country?

12 Mitchell Johnson plays for which Australian state: Queensland, Tasmania or Western Australia?

13 Which Northamptonshire left arm seamer played two Tests for England in 1993 and 1994?

14 India fielded three left arm seamers and two left arm spinners in a One Day International against Australia in 2007. Who were the five bowlers?

15 Ryan Sidebottom started his career with which county?

16 Which Pakistani left-armer made his international debut in the 2007 World Twenty20?

17 Ian Bradshaw played for which international side?

18 Which Essex left arm seamer was involved in an on-field spat with Robert Croft in a 1997 Natwest Trophy semi-final?

19 How many Test matches did Simon Brown play for England: none, one or two?

20 Wasim Akram won how many Test match caps: 99, 104 or 109?

Answers on page 220

Left Arm Spinners

QUIZ 79

1 Which English spinner's real first name is Mudhsuden?

2 Which current Australian left arm spinner took six for nine against India in 2004?

3 How many Test match wickets did Derek Underwood take: 197, 247 or 297?

4 Richard Illingworth took a wicket with his first Test match delivery. Which West Indian did he dismiss?

5 Phil Tufnell took seven wickets in a session against which country in 1992?

6 Which left arm spinner replaced Stephen Fleming as New Zealand ODI captain in 2007?

7 Which Australian left arm wrist spinner used to be a postman?

8 Which spinner took 267 Test wickets and captained India 22 times in the 1970s?

9 Which Lancashire spinner was the leading English wicket taker in the 2004 County Championship?

10 Which former England left arm spinner is now an executive with an African oil exploration company?

11 Jim Laker took 19 wickets in a Test against Australia in 1956. Which left-armer spinner took the other wicket?

12 Which current commentator took 151 Test wickets for India between 1981 and 1992?

13 Which West Indian left-arm spinner took seven wickets in the West Indies' first Test win in England in 1950?

14 Which Yorkshireman holds the record for the most First Class appearances and took an amazing 4,204 First Class wickets?

15 Who in 1992 became the first non-white to play for South Africa?

16 Ashley Giles played for which English county?

17 Which Indian born spinner played two Tests for England against India in 1996?

18 Who did Monty Panesar dismiss to claim his first Test wicket: Tendulkar, Dravid or Laxman?

19 Which South African spinner was once famously described as having a bowling action which resembled 'a frog in a blender'?

20 Which Pakistani left arm spinner took 171 Test wickets between 1976 and 1988?

Answers on page 220

Left-Handed Batsmen

1 Which stylish left-hander scored 8,231 Test runs for England between 1978 and 1992?

2 Who scored 162 on his Test debut for Australia and then went on to captain South Africa?

3 Marcus Trescothick made his highest Test score of 219 against which country?

4 Which South African played just 23 Test matches but scored 2,256 runs at an average of 60.97?

5 Which Englishman made a century in his first Test match against Australia in 1993?

6 Which Australian left-hander scored a total of 839 runs in the 1993 Ashes Series?

7 Which former England opening batsman has the middle name Verity?

8 Which South African left-hander has the nickname Biff?

9 Justin Langer captained which English county in 2007?

10 True or false: Michael Bevan never scored a Test match century?

11 Which Indian scored a century at Lord's on his Test debut in 1996?

12 Which New Zealander led Nottinghamshire to the County Championship in 2005?

13 Which Surrey batsman, who had a highest Test score of 310 not out, is one of the few Norfolk born men to play Test cricket?

14 Which West Indian batsman who scored 3,171 Test runs between 1976 and 1987, has the first name Hilary?

15 Who scored 446 runs in just three Test matches on the West Indies ill-fated tour of England in 2007?

16 Which left-hander holds the record for the highest Test score made by a wicketkeeper?

17 Who is the only man to score a Test match century which included just one boundary?

18 Which Australian had an amazing average of 79.85 after his first 16 Test matches?

19 Boof is the nickname of which former Australian batsman?

20 Which destructive Sri Lankan opener was the first cricketer to be appointed a UN Goodwill Ambassador?

Off Spinners

QUIZ 81

1 Which England off spinner took 19 wickets in a single Test match against Australia in 1953?

2 Which West Indian was the first spinner to take 300 Test wickets?

3 Brian Lara reached his World Record Test score of 400 not out by hitting which England off spinner for four?

4 Which Pakistan and Surrey spinner is credited with developing the doosra?

5 Which Scottish born off spinner took six for 67 on his Test debut for England against Australia in 1993?

6 Which Australian off spinner won a World Cup winner's medal in 2003, despite not playing a game in the competition?

7 How old was Shaun Udal when he made his Test debut: 24, 30 or 36?

8 Which Australian off spinner famously appeared in advertisements for Advanced Hair Studio: Colin Miller, Greg Matthews or Tim May?

9 Portly spinner Ramesh Powar plays for which country?

10 Which Australian off spinner turned administrator did Shane Warne place at number 31 in his list of 50 Greatest Cricketers?

11 Which Indian off spinner turned umpire took 156 Test wickets between 1965 and 1983, and is also a qualified mechanical engineer?

12 Which Yorkshire off spinner captained England to Ashes victory in 1970/71?

13 Which Indian spinner took 32 wickets in a three match series against Australia in 2001?

14 Jeetan Patel plays for which country?

15 Which off spinner played Test cricket for both Zimbabwe and South Africa but was actually born in Egypt?

16 Which South African off spinner scored a Test century while batting at number 10 against Pakistan in 1998?

17 Which England off spinner was the only man to go on both English rebel tours to South Africa in 1981/82 and 1989/90?

18 Kevin Pietersen's first two Test victims were both wicketkeepers. Can you name them?

19 Which former England off spinner is now the Chairman of Cricket at Somerset?

20 Which Surrey and England off spinner took five wickets in six balls against Sussex in 1972?

Answers on page 221

Opening Batsmen

QUIZ 82

1   Who opened the batting with Marcus Trescothick in the 2005 Ashes series?

2   Which England opening batsman was dismissed for nought 20 times in his 115 match Test career?

3   Which opening pair have put on the most Test runs in partnership together?

4   What is the highest Test score made by an opening batsman?

5   Who has scored the most Test match centuries as an opening batsman?

6   Which opening pair have put on the most One Day International runs in partnership together?

7   Which two England openers both scored centuries in a One Day International against South Africa in 2003?

8   Desmond Haynes played domestic cricket for which English county?

9   Opener Chris Gayle hit a Test match triple century against which country?

10   Who opened the batting for England alongside Graham Gooch in the 1992 World Cup?

11   Which Indian opening pair put on 410 for the first wicket in a Test match against Pakistan in 2006?

12 Which South African opener smashed scores of 277, 85 and 259 in consecutive Test innings against England in 2003?

13 Which Lancashire and England opener scored 201, 2 and 69 against India in his last three Test innings?

14 Australia's Justin Langer has played for which two English county sides?

15 True or false: Gordon Greenidge was qualified to play for England?

16 Which England opener made scores of 60 and 104 not out on his Test debut against India 2006?

17 Which Pakistani opener holds the record for the slowest Test match century ever?

18 Which England opener was dismissed for 99 in Test matches in 1993 and 1994?

19 Which Australian born England opener was run out for 199 twice in the 2005 season?

20 Geoff Boycott scored his 100th First Class century against which country?

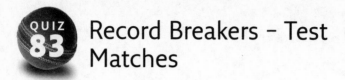

Record Breakers – Test Matches

1 The highest ever Test match innings is 952 for six declared. Which country scored it and who were the opposition?

2 Who holds the record for the highest individual innings in a Test match?

3 The highest successful fourth innings run chase is 418 for seven. Which side were the successful chasers and who were their opponents?

4 New Zealand hold the record for the lowest completed Test match innings. How many did they score: 26, 36 or 46?

5 Australia hold the record for the most consecutive Test match wins with how many: 12, 14 or 16?

6 How many consecutive matches did Bangladesh lose between November 2001 and February 2004: 19, 21 or 23?

7 Which side drew 10 consecutive matches between 1971 and 1973?

8 What is the record for the most runs scored in a single Test match day: 488, 538 or 588?

9 Pakistan hold the record for the most ducks in a Test match innings with how many: five, six or seven?

10 Which Pakistani holds the record for the most sixes in a Test match innings?

11 Who is the only man to take a five wicket haul against every Test playing nation?

12 Allan Border holds the record for the most Test match half centuries. How many did he make: 70, 80 or 90?

13 Which all rounder holds the record for taking the most wickets in an innings while captaining a Test side?

14 Who with 96 wickets in 2005 holds the record for the most Test wickets in a calendar year?

15 Who is the only man to take 19 wickets in a single Test match?

16 Which West Indian spinner holds the record for the most balls bowled in a single Test innings with 588?

17 Which Sri Lankan pair put on a mammoth partnership of 624 against South Africa in 2006?

18 Which Australian holds the record for the most catches by a non-wicketkeeper in Test matches?

19 Which Indian wicketkeeper holds the record for the most stumpings in a Test match innings?

20 Allan Border holds the record for the most consecutive Test appearances. How many did he make: 133, 143 or 153?

Answers on page 221

Record Breakers – One Day Internationals

QUIZ 84

1   What is the largest margin of victory in a One Day International: 237, 247 or 257 runs?

2   The highest ever score achieved in a One Day International, 443 for nine, was scored by which country?

3   What is the lowest innings in a One Day International: 35, 40 or 45?

4   Australia hold the record for the most consecutive One Day International wins with how many: 17, 19 or 21?

5   What is the record for the most wides in a One Day International innings: 33, 35 or 37?

6   Who with over 15,000 runs is the all time leading One Day International run scorer?

7   Which Pakistani holds the record for the highest individual score in a One Day International?

8   Which two men, one English and one West Indian, made centuries on both their first and last One Day International appearances?

9   Three players have scored centuries in three consecutive One Day Internationals. Can you name them?

10   Which all rounder holds the record for the most runs in One Day Internationals without hitting a century?

11 Who holds the record for the fastest One Day International century?

12 Sanath Jayasuriya holds the record for the fastest One Day International 50. How many deliveries did it take him?

13 Which Australian's 10 overs cost him a mammoth 113 runs against South Africa in 2006?

14 The highest partnership in a One Day International of 331 was compiled by which Indian pair?

15 Which Pakistani holds the record for the highest score by a number 11 in a One Day International?

16 Who is the only man to represent both England and Scotland in One Day Internationals?

17 Which West Indian surprisingly holds the record for the fewest runs conceded in a 10 over spell in a One Day International?

18 Who is the only Englishman to take more than 200 One Day International wickets?

19 What is the highest score by a team batting second to win a One Day International: 378, 418 or 438?

20 How many players have been dismissed Handled The Ball in One Day Internationals: none, one or two?

Answers on page 221

Smell the Leather – Pacemen

1 Which Pakistani fast bowler topped 100mph on the speed gun during the 2003 World Cup?

2 Which English batsman faced the record-breaking delivery?

3 Allan Donald was involved in a famously heated battle with which English batsman at Trent Bridge in 1998?

4 Aussie speedster Shaun Tait made his Test debut against which country?

5 Stephen Harmison took a record breaking 7-12 against which side in 2004?

6 Which English fast bowler had the nickname Typhoon?

7 Which oft injured New Zealand speedster took 74 wickets in his first 16 Test matches?

8 Who was called into the West Indies Test team after being spotted in the nets by Brian Lara, despite only having played one First Class game for Barbados?

9 Which English fast bowler hosted the TV show *Indoor League*?

10 Which bowler was known as White Lightning?

11 Who with 325 victims is second on England's all time Test wickets list?

12 Which West Indian great has the lowest bowling average of anyone to have taken at least 200 Test wickets?

13 Which Sri Lankan fast bowler is noted for his curly blond hair, eyebrow piercing and round arm action?

14 Which England paceman who played 49 Tests from 1965 to 1976, has the middle name Augustine?

15 What did Devon Malcolm say after being hit on the head by a bouncer from Fanie de Villiers at The Oval in 1994?

16 How many wickets did Malcolm take in the subsequent innings: none, six or nine?

17 Which England fast bowler had the nickname Picca?

18 Who has the best strike rate of any bowler with at least 200 Test wickets: Waqar Younis, Allan Donald or Curtly Ambrose?

19 Who was the only England paceman to take five wickets in an innings on two occasions in the 2005 Ashes series?

20 Graham Gooch has said the one time he feared for his life at the crease was when he was facing which West Indian in 1986?

Answers on page 221

Swingers and Seamers

1 Which England swing bowler took a hat-trick against the West Indies in 2004?

2 Which Australian medium pacer and bête noir of Graham Gooch took 100 of his 170 Test wickets against England?

3 Which England seamer has had a beer called The Nighwatchmen named in his honour?

4 Which Australian swinger took 16 wickets against England at Lord's in 1972?

5 Which seam bowler took 177 Test wickets for England between 1989 and 1998?

6 Which Glamorgan seamer took over 2,000 First Class wickets but never played a Test match?

7 Who took 236 Test wickets for India between 1991 and 2002 and also has a Bachelor of Engineering Degree?

8 Glen McGrath dismissed which England batsman 19 times in his Test match career?

9 Which England seamer bowled England to victory taking 6-60 against Australia in Melbourne in 1998?

10 Who took a hat-trick against Australia in Sydney in 1999?

Answers on page 221

11 Which England seamer who took 234 Test wickets was born in Christchurch, New Zealand?

12 Who in 2007 became the third South African to take 300 Test wickets?

13 Which South African swing bowler took 5-18 against England in the 2007 World Cup?

14 Which West Indian bowler was England's bowling coach on their 2007 tour to Sri Lanka?

15 Dominic Cork took a Test hat-trick against which opposition?

16 Which moustachioed Australian had the nickname Fruitfly due to his reputation as the biggest Australian pest?

17 Which former Warwickshire and Worcestershire swing bowler shares a name with a former Tottenham Hotspur captain?

18 Who is Zimbabwe's all time leading Test wicket taker?

19 Which Pakistani who took 177 Test wickets between 1969 and 1984, is said to be the father of reverse swing?

20 Which famous twin took 39 wickets in England's 1953 series with Australia?

Answers on page 221

Tail Enders

1 Tail end batsmen are often compared to which animal: rabbits, hares or stoats?

2 Which number 11 holds the record for the most not outs in Test cricket?

3 Which Australian leg spinner scored five consecutive Test match noughts in 1985?

4 Which England number 11 once forgot to take his bat out to the middle?

5 Which tail ender who has played over 30 Test matches for New Zealand, is still yet to reach double figures?

6 Azhar Mahmood put on 151 for the last wicket with which number 11 against South Africa in 1997?

7 Glen McGrath scored his only Test match half-century against which country?

8 Which regular number 11 opened the batting for Derbyshire in a match against India in 1996?

9 Which number 11 batted for 101 minutes for New Zealand against South Africa in 1999, but didn't get off the mark?

10 Who is the only nightwatchman to score a Test match double century?

11 Which number 11 was England's top scorer in the second innings of their match against South Africa at Cape Town in 2005?

12 Which last wicket pair almost stole the Edgbaston Ashes Test for Australia in 2005?

13 Which tail ender scored a crucial 16 in England's 12 run win over Australia in Melbourne in 1998?

14 Which number 11 put on a match saving 106 for the last wicket with Nathan Astle in his last Test appearance against England in 1997?

15 Which England tail ender had a One Day International batting average of 15 despite his highest score being just five not out?

16 Which Yorkshire, Northants and Sussex seamer scored only six more runs (590) than he took wickets (584)?

17 What is the highest score made by a number 11 in a Test match: 75, 85 or 95?

18 Which Indian made the highest Test score by a number 11?

19 Muttiah Muralitharan made his highest Test score of 67 against which country in 2001?

20 Who holds the record for the most Test match ducks?

Answers on page 222

QUIZ 88 West Indian Bowlers

1 Who is the leading West Indian Test wicket taker?

2 Which West Indian paceman was known as Whispering Death?

3 Which former West Indian fast bowler is a qualified airline pilot: Colin Croft, Ezra Moseley or Courtney Walsh?

4 Four West Indian bowlers have taken 300 Test wickets. Who are they?

5 Who was the first West Indian bowler to claim a Test hat-trick on Caribbean soil?

6 Two bowlers with the same surname played for the West Indies in the 1990s. Who were they?

7 Which bowler was known as Big Bird?

8 Who took 192 Test wickets between 1958 and 1969?

9 Which legendary fast bowler's first names are Anderson Montgomery Everton?

10 Wayne Daniel played for which English county?

11 Who took 14 wickets against England at the Oval in 1976?

12 Of bowlers with over two hundred Test wickets, which West Indian has the lowest average?

13 Which current commentator took 161 Test wickets between 1989 and 1998?

14 Who bowled the last over in the 1960 tied Test against Australia: Wes Hall, Garry Sobers or Charlie Griffith?

15 Which Lancashire and West Indies fast bowler who played between 1986 and 1992 has the first name Balfour?

16 Who is the only West Indian bowler to take nine wickets in a Test Match innings: Curtly Ambrose, Malcolm Marshall or Jack Noreiga?

17 Which Gloucestershire, Sussex and Nottinghamshire all rounder took 792 First Class wickets but never played a Test match?

18 Which West Indian pace bowler joined Hampshire in 2007?

19 Who are the two West Indian bowlers to have taken over two hundred One Day International wickets?

20 Sylvester Clarke spent nine seasons with which English county?

Answers on page 222

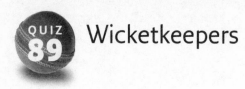

Wicketkeepers

1 Who is England's most capped Test wicketkeeper?

2 How many Test matches did Alec Stewart play as wicketkeeper: 62, 72 or 82?

3 Who was the only wicketkeeper named in the top ten of Shane Warne's 50 Greatest Cricketers?

4 Which Australian wicketkeeper shares a name with a former Fulham, QPR and Manchester City footballer?

5 Which England wicketkeeper made a century on his Test debut at Lord's in 2007?

6 What is the record for the most dismissals in a Test match innings: six, seven or eight?

7 What is the most successful bowler wicketkeeper partnership in terms of dismissals: Lillee and Marsh, Healy and Warne or Gilchrist and McGrath?

8 Who holds the record for the highest Test score by a wicketkeeper: Kumar Sangakara, Adam Gilchrist or Andy Flower?

9 What is the highest score by an England wicketkeeper: 163, 173 or 183?

10 Which Indian holds the record for the most stumpings in a Test match?

11 Which wicketkeeper played 81 Tests for the West Indies and never lost a series?

12 Geraint Jones was born in what country?

13 Which two wicketkeepers jointly hold the record for the most Test dismissals in a calendar year?

14 Which West Indian all rounder did Mark Boucher dismiss to claim his only Test wicket as a bowler?

15 What is the most dismissals by a wicketkeeper in a One Day International: five, six or seven?

16 Which former England wicketkeeper is a goalkeeping coach for Conference football side Forest Green Rovers?

17 Which bald-headed 'keeper played 88 Test matches for India from 1976 to 1986?

18 Who holds the record for the most Test dismissals by a Pakistani wicketkeeper?

19 Which current international umpire was a wicketkeeper with Middlesex and Sussex?

20 Who replaced Matt Prior as an emergency wicketkeeper for England in the World Twenty20 in 2007?

Answers on page 222

Wrist Spinners

1 Which leg spinner has taken the most Test wickets?

2 Which Englishman played two Tests for England in 2000, dropped out of First Class cricket then made his international comeback in the 2007 World Twenty20?

3 Which Pakistani leg spinner took 236 Test wickets between 1977 and 1990?

4 Which Indian leggie turned commentator took 12 wickets in his second Test match appearance but only played seven more matches?

5 Which Kenya and one time Warwickshire spinner took five for 24 against Sri Lanka in the 2003 Cricket World Cup?

6 Which Australian spinner took 27 wickets at an average of just 17.70 in the 1998/99 Ashes series?

7 Which Australian leggie turned selector made his Test debut in 1989 aged 34: Trevor Hohns or Bob Holland?

8 Which Pakistani spinner was the last man to take over one hundred First Class wickets in an English season?

9 True or false: India's Bhagwat Chandasekar took more wickets than he scored runs in Test cricket?

10 Who played four Test matches for the West Indies between 1997 and 2006 taking just one wicket at an average of 388: Rawl Lewis, Dinanath Ramnarine or Rajindra Dhanraj?

11 Which New Zealand born leg spinner played 37 Tests for Australia and is often credited with developing the flipper?

12 Which England spinner who played 18 Tests for England between 1992 and 2000, has the initials IDK?

13 Which Indian is one of only two men in Test match history to take all 10 wickets in a Test innings?

14 Danish Kaneria plays for which English county?

15 Which Yorkshire leg spinning all rounder was named the Cricket Writers' Club 2007 Young Cricketer of the Year?

16 Which 17-year-old spinner made his debut for India against England in March 2006?

17 Which Zimbabwean leg spinner played alongside his brother Brian in Test matches in the 1990s?

18 Michael Atherton claimed two Test wickets with his part-time leg spin. Who were the unfortunate victims?

19 Which English bowler is credited with inventing the googly: Bernard Bosanquet, Tich Freeman or Eric Hollies?

20 Which former Australian wrist spinner is said to be Shane Warne's spin guru?

Answers on page 222

QUIZ 91 Books

1   Which former England captain wrote a thriller called *'Testkill'*?

2   Which former England wicketkeeper's autobiography was called *'Taking it from Behind'*?

3   The award winning *'A Lot of Hard Yakka'* was written by which former Middlesex seamer?

4   *'Don't Tell Kath'* was the title of which all rounder's autobiography?

5   Which England spinner wrote a diary of a tour to the Caribbean called *'Postcards From The Beach'*?

6   The autobiography of which former England coach was called *'Behind the Shades'*?

7   In what year was the first *'Wisden Cricketers' Almanack'* published: 1864, 1874 or 1884?

8   Which Glamorgan and England batsman released an autobiography called *'Third Man to Fatty's Leg'*?

9   *'Out of my Comfort Zone'* was written by which Australian captain?

10   Which Warwickshire all rounder's autobiography was called *'Wasted: The Incredible True Story of Cricket's First Rock 'N' Roll Star'*?

11   Wasim Khan's award winning book was called *'Brimful of ...'*: Passion, Runs or Wickets?

Answers on page 222

12 *'The Flame Still Burns'* is a biography of which former Warwickshire, Somerset and Glamorgan medium pacer?

13 The biography of which West Indian legend was called *'Supercat'*?

14 Nasser Hussain's autobiography was subtitled *'Playing With ...'*: England, Fire or Essex?

15 Gideon Haigh's *'Mystery Spinner'* told the story of which extraordinary Australian bowler?

16 Who wrote a diary called *'Eight Days a Week'*?

17 *'Portrait of a Flawed Genius'* is the title of a biography about which player?

18 Who wrote the seminal *'The Art of Captaincy'*?

19 Which former England coach's autobiography was subtitled *'Anything But Murder'*?

20 Which umpire's autobiography is one of the biggest selling sports books of all time?

Answers on page 222

Grounds

QUIZ 92

1 The first ever Test match was played at which ground: Lord's, the Melbourne Cricket Ground or The Oval?

2 Which English county play their home games at Grace Road?

3 The Radcliffe Road End can be found at which English Test venue?

4 Eden Gardens can be found in which country?

5 The Riverside in Durham hosted its first Test match in 2003. Who were England's opponents?

6 At which ground is the Boxing Day Test in Australia traditionally held?

7 Newlands is in which South African city: Cape Town, Durban or Pretoria?

8 The Basin Reserve can be found in which country?

9 A tree can be found in the outfield of which English county ground?

10 What are the names of the two ends at Lord's?

11 What is the name of the coastal wind which famously blows on to the WACA at Perth?

12 The first ever FA Cup final was played at which Test venue?

13 Which Football League venue has also hosted a Test match?

14 Sabina Park can be found on which West Indian island?

15 The fastest Test century ever and the highest individual Test innings were both scored at which ground?

16 The Gaddafi Stadium is in which country: Libya, Pakistan or UAE?

17 Who plays their home games at Sophia Gardens?

18 Which English county play some of their home games at Whitgift School?

19 The Wankhede Stadium is in which Indian city: Mumbai, Hyderabad or New Delhi?

20 Which English Test venue backs onto a rugby league ground?

Answers on page 222

Language of Cricket

QUIZ 93

1 A person who is out for nought has scored: a duck, a chook or a rook?

2 Which of the following isn't a fielding position: third man, fine leg or third leg?

3 An unplayable delivery is said to be: a jaffa, an orange or a satsuma?

4 A 'Michelle' is slang for taking how many wickets: four, five or six?

5 The score of 111 has a nickname related to which British Lord?

6 What are sundries more commonly known as in England?

7 What is a googly: a fielding position, a ball delivered by a wrist spinner or a type of batting stroke?

8 What type of bowlers are likely to get excited at the prospect of bowling on a 'bunsen': spinners or seamers?

9 A delivery that doesn't bounce before it reaches the batsman is: a full toss, a long hop or a half tracker?

10 What is a groundsman more commonly known as in Australia?

11 A leg slide slog is often aimed at: cow corner, pig corner or cat corner?

12 What type of delivery is said to be named after Ellis 'Puss' Achong?

13 What is a featherbed: a flat pitch which is easy to bat on, a pitch good for bowlers or a lush green outfield?

14 In Australia what is a wrong 'un?

15 In Australia what is said to be the Devil's number: 78, 87 or 97?

16 What type of delivery comes from the Hindi-Urdu word for other: bosie, googly or doosra?

17 What is a Chinese cut: an inside edge, an outside edge or a top edge?

18 Foreign players who aren't classified as overseas players take their name from which Slovak handball player: Kolpak, Koller or Dubcek?

19 What was leg theory more commonly known as in the 1930s?

20 A non-striker who is run out backing up is said to have suffered what: a Mankad, a Majid or a Mahmood?

Answers on page 223

Laws of the Game

QUIZ 94

1 What does LBW stand for?

2 How many Laws of Cricket are there: 32, 42 or 52?

3 How many ways can a batsman be dismissed?

4 Name all the ways that a batsman can be dismissed.

5 How many runs have been scored when an umpire raises both hands above his head?

6 How much does a cricket ball weigh?

7 In Test matches how many overs must be bowled before a new ball is offered: 75, 80 or 85?

8 What is the maximum width of bat allowed: 4¼ in or 5¼ in?

9 What is signified if an umpire touches his raised knee with his hand?

10 If the ball hits an unworn helmet in the field how many runs are the batting side awarded?

11 What signal does an umpire make to signify a wide?

12 How many balls are there in an over?

13 What is the name of the formula used to decide the outcome of rain-affected matches?

14 In a five day Test match, a side must have a first innings lead of how many runs to make a side follow on: 150, 200 or 250?

15 True or false: players are allowed to use aluminium bats?

16 How tall is a full size stump: 26 in, 27 in or 28 in?

17 How wide should the set of three stumps be positioned: 8, 9 or 10 in?

18 What signal does an umpire give to signify 'one short'?

19 How long is a cricket pitch?

20 What is a beamer: a head high delivery which reaches the batsman without bouncing, a really short bouncer or a flash player's car?

QUIZ 95 Politics

1 Which former British prime minister wrote a history of cricket called *'More Than a Game'*?

2 Who is the only British prime minister to play First Class cricket?

3 Prime Minister Gordon Brown's Parliamentary Private Secretary shares a name with which former Lancashire bowler: Ian Austin, Jack Simmons or Colin Croft?

4 South Africa were banned from world cricket after their government made it clear that which England player would not be welcome?

5 In what year did South Africa make their return to international cricket: 1991, 1992 or 1993?

6 Who said 'I want everyone to play cricket in Zimbabwe; I want ours to be a nation of gentlemen'?

7 Which politician did Mark Taylor once describe as 'a cricket tragic'?

8 Which British prime minister had a news wire installed at 10 Downing Street to keep him up to date with the cricket scores?

9 Which former Pakistan all rounder has gone on to a career in politics?

10 England's match against the West Indies in 1980/81 was cancelled after the Guyanese government refused a visa to which England seamer?

11 Who captained the ill-fated England rebel tour to South Africa in 1990?

12 What did New Zealand prime minister Brian Muldoon describe as 'the most disgusting thing I can recall in the history of cricket'?

13 Who wrote the classic book on cricket, politics and colonialism, *'Beyond A Boundary'*?

14 Which former England captain stood against future Prime Minister James Callaghan in the 1964 General Election?

15 Which two Zimbabwean players wore black armbands during the 2003 Cricket World Cup 'mourning the death of democracy' in their country?

16 Which West Indian was Trinidad's first High Commissioner in London and later sat in the House of Lords?

17 Which Jamaican prime minister wrote the definitive *'A History of West Indies Cricket'*?

18 Who captained the Australian rebel tours to South Africa in the 1980s?

19 Which Trinidad and Tobago and West Indies wicketkeeper went on to become a diplomat at the United Nations?

20 True or false: in 1997 a team of Eurosceptic MPs captained by John Redwood played a team of Europhiles captained by Lord Archer?

Answers on page 223

Television

1   In what decade was live cricket first shown in England: 1920s, 1930s or 1940s?

2   Which former Hamsphire all rounder presents Channel Five's cricket coverage?

3   Which two cricketers have appeared on the BBC's 'Strictly Come Dancing'?

4   Who was the first BBC Television cricket correspondent?

5   What was the name of the cricket themed sitcom which aired on ITV between 1994 and 1996?

6   What is the name of The Analyst on Channel Five?

7   In what year was the first England overseas tour televised live: 1986, 1990 or 1994?

8   What was the name of the theme tune to BBC Cricket?

9   Which former Hampshire, Sussex, Warwickshire and Sussex seamer now provides expert analysis on a television poker show?

10 Which Kent batsman finished runner-up in the Sky Sports Poker Challenge?

11 Which former New Zealand wicketkeeper also commentates on rugby union?

12 Who resigned from the Channel 4 commentary team after admitting to a drug problem?

13 Which Australian commentator is famous for his cries of 'Got him, yes!'?

14 True or false: Peter West went to the same school as fellow sports commentators Brian Moore and Barry Davies?

15 Anita Rani and Simon Thomas present which cricket magazine show?

16 Which Welshman was the face of BBC Cricket in the 1990s?

17 Which former Lancashire seamer hosts *'Cricket Writers On TV'*?

18 In what year did Richie Benaud make his BBC Television debut: 1963, 1973 or 1983?

19 True or false: Charles Colville played First Class cricket for Surrey?

20 In 1999 which former *Top of the Pops* host became the first woman to present cricket on TV?

Answers on page 223

Test Match Special

1 In what decade was cricket commentary first heard on British radio: 1920s, 1930s or 1940s?

2 Who is the current BBC cricket correspondent?

3 In what decade did 'Test Match Special' first appear on the radio?

4 Up to the early 1990s 'Test Match Special' was broadcast on which radio station?

5 Which TMS commentator is noted for his love of pigeons and double-decker buses?

6 What is scorer Bill Frindall's nickname: Billbo Baggins, The Freckle or The Bearded Wonder?

7 Which TMS commentator memorably described Asif Mahmood's run up as like 'Groucho Marx chasing a pretty waitress'?

8 Who was the producer of 'Test Match Special' from 1973 to 2007?

9 Which TMS regular was known as The Alderman?

10 Which former TMS commentator now broadcasts UEFA Champions League games for ITV and also covered the 2007 Rugby World Cup?

11 According to Brian Johnston, who famously 'couldn't quite get his leg over'?

Answers on page 223

12 The cricket correspondent of *The Times* is also a regular on TMS. What is his name?

13 Which West Indian made his TMS debut at Headingley in 1966?

14 Which two former England internationals made their TMS debuts in 2007?

15 True or false: at Brian Johnston's memorial service at Westminster Abbey, the congregation left the church with the organist playing the theme to Australian soap *Home and Away*?

16 Who in 1998 became the first female TMS commentator?

17 Which former England all rounder and regular TMS summariser had the nickname Boil?

18 Which TMS commentator spent three years in a Japanese prisoner of war camp during the Second World War?

19 The TMS podcast usually features Jonathan Agnew in conversation with which straight-talking Yorkshireman?

20 True or false: Hugh Cornwell of punk band The Stranglers, Harry Potter actor Daniel Radcliffe and The Archbishop of Canterbury have all appeared on TMS?

Answers on page 223

Trophies and Awards

1 The Ashes is contested by which two countries?

2 Which two sides compete for the Wisden Trophy?

3 The Frank Worrell Trophy is contested between which two Test sides?

4 The trophy awarded to the winners of a series between Australia and India is named after which two legendary batsmen?

5 How tall is the Ashes urn: 4 in, 12 in or 4 ft?

6 It is thought that the Ashes in the urn are the burnt remains of what: a bail, a stump or a bat?

7 What is the name of the trophy given to the player who scores the fastest First Class century in an English season?

8 The trophy awarded to the winners of the three match One Day Series between Australia and New Zealand is named after which two cricketing families?

9 The ICC Cricketer of the Year is awarded which trophy: The Garfield Sobers Trophy, The Donald Bradman Trophy or The Viv Richards Trophy?

10 Who is the only player to win the ICC Cricketer of the Year award in consecutive years?

Answers on page 224

11 The Irani Trophy is a competition in which country?

12 Which Oscar winning film director played at Lord's in 1997?

13 Which Australian speedster was named as the ICC Emerging Player of the Year in 2007?

14 Which two England players were named in the ICC World Test Team of the Year in 2007?

15 The Patron's Trophy is a competition in which country: India, Pakistan or Sri Lanka?

16 Which prolific Pakistani batsman was the ICC Test Player of the Year in 2007?

17 The 2007 English County Championship was sponsored by which Friendly Society?

18 The Ashes urn is on display in the museum at which Test ground?

19 The SuperSport Series takes place in which country: South Africa, New Zealand or Australia?

20 The domestic competition in the West Indies originally took its name from which oil company?

Answers on page 224

Umpires

1 Which West Indian umpire holds the record for standing in the most Test matches?

2 Who were the two umpires involved in the abandoned Test between England and Pakistan in 2006?

3 Which current umpire played two Test matches for England in 1992 taking 10 wickets against Pakistan?

4 Which umpire stood in the first three World Cup Finals?

5 Aleem Dar is from which country?

6 Mike Gatting had his infamous argument with which Pakistani umpire?

7 Which umpire is noted for his crooked finger?

8 Which Australian was named ICC Umpire of the Year in 2004, 2005, 2006 and 2007?

9 Who was famous for his 'hop, skip and jump' when the scored reached 111?

10 Which India and Derbyshire spinner played 57 Test matches before going on to umpire in a further 73 Tests?

11 Which Yorkshire born umpire scored a century on his Test debut for England against West Indies in 1969?

12 Harold 'Dickie' Bird played for which two English counties?

13 True or false: Steve Bucknor once refereed a football World Cup qualifier?

14 Who were the two umpires in the 2007 Cricket World Cup final?

15 Which former Premier League football referee is now on the ECB Umpiring A list: Martin Bodenham, Vic Callow or Graham Poll?

16 Peter Willey played for which two counties?

17 Umpire Daryl Harper is from which country?

18 True or false: Steve Bucknor used to be a mathematics teacher?

19 Who umpired his first Test match in 1971 and his final ODI 30 years later in 2001?

20 Asoka de Silva is from which country?

Women's Cricket

QUIZ 100

1 In what year was the first Women's Cricket World Cup held: 1973, 1983 or 1993?

2 In what decade did England Women make their first tour to Australia and New Zealand: 1930s, 1950s or 1970s?

3 Which two countries are Test nations in Women's cricket but not in the men's game?

4 How many matches have Australia lost out of the 55 matches they have played in the Women's World Cup: five, seven or nine?

5 How many times have England been Women's World Champions: never, once or twice?

6 In what year will the next Women's World Cup be held?

7 In what country will the tournament be held?

8 Which team competed in all three World Cup finals between 1993 and 2000?

9 The wife of which legendary all rounder played for the New Zealand women's team?

10 Twins Rosemary and Elizabeth Signal played for which country?

11 How old was Charlotte Edwards when she made her England debut: 15, 16 or 17?

12 Which former England women's captain regularly appeared on Channel Four's cricket coverage?

13 Who became the first woman to run the Australian Centre of Excellence in Brisbane: Karen Ralton, Belinda Clark or Cathryn Fitzpatrick?

14 ICC Player of the Year 2007 Jhulan Goswami is from which country?

15 Which two countries toured England in 2007?

16 What is the highest score in a Women's One Day International: 355, 405 or 455?

17 Which former England women's cricketer was also a director of Wolverhampton Wanderers Football Club?

18 In what year were women finally allowed to join MCC?

19 Who did Australia beat to claim the 2005 World Cup?

20 England's women won the 2005 Ashes for the first time in how many years: 22, 32 or 42?

Answers on page 224

The Ashes Answers

Page 8

1 1877 **2** Australia 5-0 England **3** Chris Broad **4** Raymond Illingworth **5** Robin Smith **6** Matthew Hoggard **7** Rick Darling **8** The MCG and Lord's **9** George Davis **10** Warwick Armstrong **11** Bert Ironmonger **12** Len Hutton **13** David Hookes **14** Mark Taylor and Steve Waugh **15** 903 for seven by England in 1938 **16** It was exactly the same as the first match as Australia won by 45 runs **17** Ian Botham **18** None – he lost all five **19** Mark Butcher **20** Sophia Gardens, Cardiff

The Ashes 1981 Answers

Page 10

1 Australia **2** Nought in both innings **3** Mike Brearley **4** Ian Botham **5** 227 **6** 149 not out **7** Graham Dilley **8** '... the confectionery stall and out again' **9** 130 **10** Eight for 43 **11** Ian Botham **12** 118 **13** Paul Allott **14** Paul Parker **15** Allan Border **16** Terry Alderman **17** Allan Knott, Paul Downton and Bob Taylor **18** Ian Botham, Bob Willis, Geoff Boycott and Mike Gatting **19** Ian Botham and Allan Border **20** True

The Ashes 2005

Page 12

1 England 2-1 Australia **2** Ricky Ponting and Michael Vaughan **3** Australia **4** Kevin Pietersen **5** Glen McGrath **6** Two runs **7** Michael Vaughan and Andrew Strauss **8** Brett Lee and Glenn McGrath **9** Simon Jones **10** Gary Pratt **11** Matthew Hoggard **12** Shaun Tait **13** Andrew Strauss **14** 44 **15** Kevin Pietersen **16** Kevin Pietersen, Marcus Trescothick and Andrew Flintoff **17** 40 **18** Just 12 **19** Marcus Trescothick **20** Andrew Flintoff

1975 Cricket World Cup Answers

Page 14

1 England **2** West Indies **3** Australia **4** 8 **5** True **6** Sunil Gavaskar **7** Dennis Amiss **8** Glen Turner **9** Bishan Bedi **10** 17 **11** Andy Roberts **12** Viv Richards **13** Vanburn Holder **14** Gary Gilmour **15** True **16** Clive Lloyd **17** True **18** Viv Richards, Andy Roberts and Gordon Greenidge **19** Alvin Kallicharran **20** Prudential

1979 Cricket World Cup Answers

Page 16

1 England **2** West Indies **3** England **4** False **5** Collis King **6** Canada **7** Viv Richards **8** Joel Garner **9** India **10** Chris Old **11** Gordon Greenidge **12** Allan Border **13** Mike Brearley **14** True **15** 60 **16** Graham Gooch **17** 92 runs **18** Geoff Boycott **19** Mike Hendrick **20** Eight

1983 Cricket World Cup Answers

Page 18

1 England **2** India **3** West Indies **4** 38 **5** Chris Tavare **6** Graeme Hick **7** Kapil Dev **8** Paul Allott **9** England **10** Bob Willis **11** Duncan Fletcher **12** Graeme Fowler **13** Roger Binny with 18 **14** Abdul Qadir **15** Ian Gould **16** Ken MacLeay **17** David Gower **18** 183 **19** Madan Lal **20** Mohinder Amarnath

1987 Cricket World Cup

1 India and Pakistan **2** 50 **3** Australia **4** England **5** Viv Richards
6 India **7** Allan Border dismissed Mike Gatting **8** The first hat-trick
9 Graham Gooch **10** A reverse sweep **11** West Indies **12** Craig
McDermott **13** John Emburey and Eddie Hemmings **14** Greg Dyer
15 Calcutta **16** Derek Pringle **17** David Boon **18** Gladstone Small
19 Steve Waugh and Tom Moody **20** Seven runs

Page 20

1992 Cricket World Cup Answers

1 True **2** Australia and New Zealand **3** South Africa **4** Pakistan
5 England **6** Eddo Brandes **7** Dipak Patel **8** Dermot Reeve
9 Derek Pringle **10** West Indies **11** Ian Botham **12** Martin Crowe
13 Javed Miandad **14** Wasim Akram **15** True **16** 39 **17** The MCG
18 Inzamam-ul-Haq **19** Alec Stewart **20** Hick, Smith, Lamb, Lewis,
Reeve, Pringle, DeFreitas, Small

Page 22

1996 Cricket World Cup Answers

1 India, Pakistan and Sri Lanka **2** Sri Lanka **3** Australia **4** Gary Kirsten
5 Netherlands, United Arab Emirates and Kenya **6** Graeme Hick
7 West Indies and Australia **8** Sri Lanka **9** Kenya **10** Neil Smith
11 66/1 **12** Anil Kumble **13** Chris Harris **14** Lahore **15** Sachin
Tendulkar **16** One **17** West Indies **18** Aravinda de Silva **19** Michael
Atherton **20** Phil DeFreitas, Neil Fairbrother, Graeme Hick, Richard
Illingworth, Dermot Reeve, Robin Smith and Alec Stewart

Page 24

1999 Cricket World Cup Answers

1 Australia **2** Pakistan **3** France **4** Ian Austin **5** Scotland and
Bangladesh **6** Rahul Dravid **7** Caprice **8** Herschelle Gibbs **9** True
10 Lance Klusener **11** South Africa **12** Bangladesh **13** Prasad
14 New Zealand **15** Sourav Ganguly **16** Geoff Allott **17** Extras
18 Shane Warne **19** Alec Stewart **20** Darren Gough

Page 26

2003 Cricket World Cup Answers

1 South Africa **2** Australia **3** India **4** 125 runs **5** Craig Wishart with
172 **6** Sachin Tendulkar **7** Chaminda Vaas **8** Andy Bichel **9** Sri
Lanka **10** John Davison **11** Australia, India, Sri Lanka and Kenya
12 New Zealand **13** England **14** Canada **15** Sri Lanka, Bangladesh
and Zimbabwe **16** Ricky Ponting **17** Sri Lanka **18** Amazingly against
Australia **19** Bangladesh, England, Pakistan, South Africa and West
Indies **20** Johannesburg

Page 28

2007 Cricket World Cup Answers

1 West Indies **2** Australia **3** Sri Lanka **4** Bob Woolmer **5** Ireland
6 Ed Joyce **7** Bangladesh **8** Adam Gilchrist **9** South Africa
10 Matthew Hayden **11** Herschelle Gibbs **12** The Netherlands' Dan
van Bunge **13** Ireland **14** Lasith Malinga **15** Steve Bucknor
16 Mark Boucher broke the record and was subsequently beaten by
Brendon McCullum **17** Dwayne Leverock **18** Glen McGrath **19** India
scored 413 for five against Bermuda **20** Inzamam-ul-Haq, Brian Lara,
Sachin Tendulkar, Sanath Jayasuriya and Anderson Cummins

Page 30

World Twenty20 2007 Answers

QUIZ 13

Page 32

1 South Africa **2** India **3** Pakistan **4** Irfan Pathan **5** Umar Gul **6** Five runs **7** India **8** Brett Lee **9** India and Pakistan **10** Zimbabwe **11** Matthew Hayden **12** Chris Gayle **13** Yuvraj Singh **14** Stuart Broad **15** Sri Lanka **16** Bangladesh **17** Sanath Jayasuriya **18** Mark Gillespie **19** Craig McMillan **20** Chris Gayle hit 10 against South Africa

English Domestic Competitions Answers

QUIZ 14

Page 34

1 Surrey **2** Lancashire **3** 1963 **4** Sussex **5** Leicestershire **6** Lancashire **7** Wayne Daniel **8** Lancashire **9** 57 by Essex in 1996 **10** Glamorgan **11** Durham **12** Yorkshire **13** Leicestershire and Glamorgan **14** Sussex **15** Brian Langford **16** Warwickshire **17** Gloucestershire **18** John Hampshire and Barry Dudleston **19** Graham Rose **20** Ben Hollioake

English Twenty20 Cup Answers

QUIZ 15

Page 36

1 Kent **2** Gloucestershire **3** Ryan McLaren **4** Lancashire and Sussex **5** Lance Klusener **6** Luke Wright **7** Murali Kartik **8** Somerset **9** Sussex with 67 and 68 **10** Leicestershire **11** Cameron White **12** Surrey **13** Andrew Symonds **14** 14 **15** Tim Murtagh **16** Matthew Hoggard **17** Dimitri Mascarenhas **18** All Saints **19** The Rose Bowl **20** Adam Hollioake at 9.6

India versus Australia 2001 Answers

QUIZ 16

Page 38

1 India won 2-1 **2** Australia won by 10 wickets **3** Michael Slater **4** Harbhajan Singh **5** 274 **6** Steve Waugh **7** V.S. Laxman **8** V.S. Laxman and Rahul Dravid **9** 657 **10** Harbhajan Singh **11** Sachin Tendulkar **12** Matthew Hayden **13** Harbhajan Singh **14** Two wickets **15** Steve Waugh **16** Shane Warne **17** Adam Gilchrist **18** Amazingly just three **19** Glenn McGrath **20** Steve Waugh and Sourav Ganguly

Sheffield Shield Answers

QUIZ 17

Page 40

1 Six **2** New South Wales **3** Tasmania **4** Matthew Elliott **5** Pura **6** Darren Lehmann **7** Michael Bevan **8** False – he averaged an amazing 110.19 **9** Colin Miller **10** Queensland **11** 1981/82 **12** Jamie Cox **13** Jack Simmons **14** Barry Richards **15** 1,107 **16** Western Australia **17** 68 years **18** New South Wales **19** Queensland **20** South Australia

World Series Cricket Answers

QUIZ 18

Page 42

1 Kerry Packer **2** 1977 **3** Tony Greig **4** The Australians, West Indies and Rest of the World **5** Ian Chappell **6** Dennis Amiss **7** David Hookes **8** Eight **9** Dennis Lillee **10** Yellow **11** Barry Richards, Eddie Barlow, Garth le Roux, Clive Rice and Mike Procter **12** Allan Knott **13** Australian Rules football **14** Clive Lloyd **15** A drop in pitch **16** True **17** Geoff Boycott **18** True **19** *C'mon Aussie C'mon* **20** True

Ambrose and Walsh Answers

1 Antigua **2** Northamptonshire **3** Australia **4** 43 **5** 491
6 Gloucestershire **7** Australia **8** Dean Jones **9** A then record 519
10 True **11** Michael Atherton **12** Dermot Reeve **13** Richie
Richardson **14** False – Ambrose plays in the band **15** England
16 Jamiaca **17** Elconn Lynwall **18** 405 **19** 1987 **20** True

Page 44

Allan Border Answers

1 156 **2** 205 **3** Essex and Gloucestershire **4** Four **5** 1985
6 Mike Brearley **7** True **8** Kim Hughes **9** Twice **10** Christian Vieri
11 Pakistan **12** 1987 **13** Neil Foster **14** Queensland **15** 27
16 Score 150 in each innings **17** Durban **18** True **19** 93 **20** AB

Page 46

Sir Ian Botham Answers

1 Somerset, Worcestershire and Durham **2** Australia **3** 149 not out
4 Scunthorpe United **5** 383 **6** Merv Hughes **7** Greg Chappell
8 Take 10 wickets and score a century **9** Queensland **10** Shredded
Wheat **11** Terence **12** 208 **13** True **14** None **15** *A Question of
Sport* **16** Joel Garner **17** Pakistan **18** He admitted taking cannabis
19 1981 **20** True

Page 48

Geoffrey Boycott Answers

1 Yorkshire **2** Surrey **3** True **4** 22 **5** Australia **6** Greg Chappell
7 True **8** Ian Botham **9** 16 **10** Graham Gooch **11** Graeme Pollock
12 Michael Parkinson **13** 41 **14** Derek Randall **15** Manchester
United **16** Dominic Cork **17** Fiery **18** 47.72 **19** Twice
20 Northern Transvaal

Page 50

Sir Donald Bradman Answers

1 52 **2** 334 **3** Headingley **4** True **5** 99:94 **6** Eric Hollies **7** New
South Wales and South Australia **8** Hugo Weaving **9** False – Brian
Lara has too **10** 974 **11** Two **12** 39 **13** 12 **14** George **15** 1949
16 True **17** True **18** Hedley Verity **19** 'I wish I could bat like that'
20 452 not out

Page 52

Andrew Flintoff Answers

1 Lancashire **2** South Africa **3** Fred Flintstone **4** Jacques Kallis
5 New Zealand **6** Nine **7** Pedalo **8** Alex Tudor **9** True **10** 167
11 Just three **12** Neil Fairbrother **13** The Oval **14** Tino Best
15 True **16** Jacques Kallis **17** He doesn't have a middle name
18 2005 **19** 402 **20** 20

Page 54

Brian Lara Answers

1 Trinidad **2** Warwickshire **3** Pakistan **4** Australia **5** Allan Border
6 Dwight Yorke **7** True **8** Nine **9** Chris Lewis **10** True **11** England
12 Exeter **13** 501 not out **14** Durham **15** Northern Transvaal
16 Charles **17** Glen McGrath with 15 **18** 52.89 **19** Courtney Walsh
20 Robin Peterson

Page 56

Lillee and Thomson Answers

1 355 **2** True **3** Alan Knott on 12 occasions **4** Also Alan Knott
5 Western Australia and Tasmania **6** 200 **7** Northamptonshire **8** 33
9 95 **10** Middlesex **11** John Edrich **12** True **13** 70 **14** David Lloyd
15 73 not out **16** Chennai (Madras) **17** False – the song featured
Dennis Lillee **18** Javed Miandad **19** Graham Gooch **20** Keith

Page 58

Muttiah Muralitharan Answers

1 Sri Lanka **2** 1992 **3** Craig McDermott **4** Darrell Hair **5** Lancashire and
Kent **6** False: Jim Laker did too **7** Courtney Walsh **8** Bangladesh **9** Mark
Boucher **10** England **11** Two **12** 67 **13** Steve Waugh **14** Alec Stewart
was run out **15** None – he missed the competition through injury
16 True **17** Kevin Pietersen **18** 23 **19** True **20** John Howard

Page 60

Kevin Pietersen Answers

1 South Africa **2** Australia **3** 57 **4** Nottinghamshire **5** 10
6 False – he's been dismissed for 158 three times **7** West Indies
8 Kamran Akmal **9** Liberty X **10** Six **11** Three **12** Paul Collingwood
13 Muttiah Muralitharan **14** True **15** Hampshire **16** 116
17 Glen McGrath **18** None **19** Zimbabwe **20** True

Page 62

Sir Viv Richards Answers

1 Antigua **2** India **3** 1979 **4** 56 **5** Isaac Vivian Alexander Richards
6 1999 **7** Glamorgan **8** 50 **9** True **10** Dean Jones **11** True
12 291 **13** Queensland **14** 189 not out **15** 24 **16** 1976
17 David Lawrence **18** True **19** Dennis Lillee **20** True

Page 64

Sir Garfield Sobers Answers

1 Left-handed **2** Barbados **3** 17 **4** 365 not out **5** Nottinghamshire
6 True **7** Swansea **8** 235 **9** Frank Worrell **10** 1975 **11** 26
12 St Aubrun **13** South Australia **14** 93 **15** True – in Barbados in
1966 **16** 57.78 **17** Rohan Kanhai **18** Derek Underwood
19 Alan Knott **20** True

Page 66

Sachin Tendulkar Answers

1 16 **2** Yorkshire **3** Vinod Kambli **4** Waqar Younis **5** England **6** 17
7 True **8** Bangladesh **9** True **10** True **11** 79 **12** Mohammad
Azharuddin **13** Sunil Gavaskar **14** John McEnroe **15** Merv Hughes
16 1997 **17** True **18** South Africa **19** 1996 and 2003 **20** True

Page 68

Michael Vaughan Answers

1 Yorkshire **2** South Africa **3** Two for four **4** Nasser Hussain
5 Sachin Tendulkar **6** 197 **7** True **8** Sheffield Wednesday **9** 2002
10 One **11** Ricky Ponting **12** Australia **13** New Zealand, West Indies
and South Africa **14** Peter May **15** West Indies **16** 2007 **17** Virgil
18 Pakistan **19** True **20** 2003

Page 70

Shane Warne Answers

1 Ravi Shastri **2** 708 **3** Mike Gatting **4** Daniel Vettori **5** Hampshire
6 Alec Stewart **7** 99 **8** 96 **9** Dennis Lillee **10** Two **11** Devon
Malcolm **12** St Kilda **13** Andrew Flintoff **14** False **15** Victoria
16 True **17** England **18** Sachin Tendulkar **19** 12 **20** Baked beans

Page 72

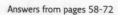

Wasim and Waqar Answers

1 1985 against New Zealand **2** Wasim with 414 took more than Waqar with 373 **3** Lancashire **4** False – he was known as Burewala Express **5** Three **6** Wasim **7** Surrey and Glamorgan **8** 1992 **9** 257 not out **10** 2003 **11** 1993 **12** 1991 **13** Brian Lara **14** Sri Lanka both times **15** True **16** 45 **17** Sanjay Manjrekar **18** True **19** Ian Botham, Chris Lewis and Alan Lamb **20** Nick Knight

Page 74

Australia Answers

1 Green **2** Michael Clarke **3** Brett Lee **4** Bob Massie **5** Don Bradman **6** Michael Slater **7** Yellow **8** Dennis Lillee **9** Rashid Latif **10** Tom Moody **11** West Indies **12** 380 by Matthew Hayden **13** Six **14** Shane Warne **15** Mike Hussey **16** Steve Waugh **17** West Indies and India **18** New Zealand **19** Steve Waugh **20** Melbourne

Page 76

Bangladesh Answers

1 Tigers **2** 2000 **3** Aminul Islam **4** 1999 **5** Pakistan **6** 35 **7** India **8** Zimbabwe **9** Mohammad Ashraful **10** Enamul Haque Jr **11** Sri Lanka **12** Mohammad Rafique **13** India and South Africa **14** Kenya and West Indies **15** Dav Whatmore **16** True **17** Mohammad Ashraful **18** Sri Lanka **19** The Riverside, Durham **20** Gordon Greenidge

Page 78

England Answers

1 Nasser Hussain **2** Graham Gooch **3** Alec Stewart **4** Paul Collingwood **5** Graham Thorpe **6** Alex Tudor **7** David Gower **8** Geoff Boycott **9** Len Hutton **10** Mark Butcher **11** Ronnie Irani **12** Ian Botham **13** Alastair Cook, Paul Collingwood, Ian Bell, Matt Prior and Kevin Pietersen **14** They all won just a single One Day International cap **15** Richard Johnson **16** They dismissed Steve Waugh **17** Sir Pelham Warner **18** Andrew Caddick **19** Michael Vaughan **20** Alec Stewart, Graham Gooch, David Gower, Michael Atherton, Colin Cowdrey, Geoff Boycott, Ian Botham and Graham Thorpe

Page 80

India Answers

1 Blue **2** Mahendra Singh Dhoni **3** Virender Sehwag **4** 1930s **5** Madan Lal **6** Harbhajan Singh **7** Anil Kumble **8** Rahul Dravid, Sachin Tendulkar and Virender Sehwag **9** Lancashire **10** Sachin Tendulkar **11** Zaheer Abbas **12** 1971 **13** True **14** Kapil Dev **15** True **16** Bhagwat Chandrasekhar **17** Kris Srikkanth **18** Kolkata (formerly Calcutta) **19** Sourav Ganguly **20** Syed Kirmani

Page 82

New Zealand Answers

1 Grey **2** Peter Petherick **3** Five times **4** South Africa **5** 1930s **6** 1978 **7** Martin Crowe **8** Mark Greatbatch **9** Richard Hadlee **10** Jacob Oram **11** Chris Martin **12** Danny Morrison **13** 18 **14** Richard Hadlee, Chris Cairns and Daniel Vettori **15** 26 **16** 40 **17** Chris Cairns and Chris Harris **18** Bert Sutcliffe **19** Geoff Allott **20** Christchurch

Page 84

Pakistan Answers

1 Green **2** 1950s **3** Geoff Lawson **4** Mohammad Yousuf **5** Uncle Cricket **6** Javed Miandad, Mohammad Yousuf and Inzamam-ul-Haq **7** Abdul Qadir **8** Javed Miandad **9** Saeed Anwar **10** Wasim Akram, Abdul Razzaq and Mohammad Sami **11** True **12** Zaheer Abbas **13** 48 **14** Hanif Mohammad and Inzamam-ul-Haq **15** Australia **16** Javed Miandad and Inzamam-ul-Haq **17** 1987 **18** 1992 and 1999 **19** Wasim Akram **20** West Indies

South Africa Answers

1 Green **2** 1990s **3** Jacques Kallis **4** Mark Boucher **5** True **6** 1889 **7** Never **8** Ashwell Prince **9** Shaun Pollock, Allan Donald and Makhaya Ntini **10** Darryl Cullinan **11** Graeme Pollock **12** The Proteas **13** Johannesburg **14** Hansie Cronje **15** As a mark of respect to Hansie Cronje who wore the number five shirt **16** Gloucestershire **17** Jacques Kallis, Gary Kirsten and Herschelle Gibbs **18** Makhaya Ntini with four **19** Kepler Wessels **20** 22

Sri Lanka Answers

1 Blue **2** Trevor Bayliss **3** Chaminda Vaas **4** Sanath Jayasuriya **5** 1982 **6** Muttiah Muralitharan **7** Sanath Jayasuriya, Mahela Jayawardene and Aravinda de Silva **8** Marvan Atapattu **9** Chaminda Vaas **10** Nuwan Zoysa **11** Lasith Malinga **12** Kumar Sangakkara **13** Russel Arnold **14** Duleep Mendis **15** Asoka de Silva **16** Arjuna Ranatunga **17** Colombo **18** Kumar Sangakkara **19** Sanath Jayasuriya and Mahela Jayawardene **20** West Indies

West Indies Answers

1 Maroon **2** Shivnarine Chanderpaul **3** Clive Lloyd **4** Darren Sammy **5** Ireland **6** George Headley **7** Viv Richards and Michael Holding **8** Gordon Greenidge **9** Cameron Cuffy **10** 46 **11** 47 **12** Garry Sobers, Lawrence Rowe, Brian Lara and Chris Gayle **13** Antigua **14** 1984 and 1986 **15** Gordon Greenidge **16** Desmond Haynes **17** Roy Fredericks **18** False **19** Everton Weekes **20** Port of Spain, Trinidad

Zimbabwe Answers

1 1992 **2** They drew with India **3** Red **4** Australia **5** Duncan Fletcher **6** Eddo Brandes **7** England **8** Grant and Andy Flower **9** Paul Strang **10** Eddo Brandes **11** Henry Olonga **12** Pakistan **13** True **14** Alastair Campbell **15** Grant Flower **16** Australia **17** Andy Blignaut **18** David Houghton **19** Neil Johnson **20** Matthew Hayden

Derbyshire CCC Answers

1 The County Ground **2** The Phantoms **3** Simon Katich **4** Once **5** Kim Barnett **6** Somerset **7** Boyd Rankin **8** Ole Mortensen **9** Queen's Park **10** 1990 **11** 1993 **12** A rose **13** True **14** Bob Taylor **15** Dominic Cork **16** True **17** Geoff Miller **18** John Morris **19** Karl Krikken **20** Mohammad Azharuddin

Durham CCC Answers

1 The Riverside **2** 1992 **3** Ian Botham **4** Dean Jones **5** Otis Gibson
6 Dynamos **7** 2007 **8** Steve Harmison, Paul Collingwood and Liam
Plunkett **9** Graham Onions and Phil Mustard **10** Feethams, the
home of Darlington FC **11** David Graveney **12** Mark Waugh
13 Lumley Castle **14** Hampshire **15** Newcastle **16** Middlesex
17 True **18** Simon Brown **19** Martin Love **20** Sri Lanka

Page 98

Essex CCC Answers

1 Chelmsford **2** Essex Eagles **3** 1979 **4** True – but the Australians
did score 721 in the process **5** Graham Gooch **6** Trevor Bailey
7 Nasser Hussain **8** Surrey **9** 1981 **10** Peter Such **11** Alastair Cook
12 Swords **13** Mark Pettini **14** Surrey **15** Sir Geoff Hurst **16** Ravi
Bopara **17** Graham Gooch, Derek Pringle, Mark Ilott, Peter Such
18 False – brother Mark did though **19** Keith Fletcher **20** Six

Page 100

Glamorgan CCC Answers

1 Sophia Gardens **2** Robert Croft **3** Three **4** Bermuda **5** Alan Evans
6 Matthew Maynard **7** Simon Jones **8** Tony Cottey **9** Matthew
Maynard **10** Steve Watkin and Hugh Morris **11** Tony Lewis **12** True
13 Robert Croft **14** Don Shepherd **15** False **16** Colwyn Bay
17 Ian Bishop **18** Steve James **19** Malcolm Nash
20 Glamorgan Dragons

Page 102

Gloucestershire CCC Answers

1 Gladiators **2** Three times **3** Mike Smith **4** W.G. Grace **5** Wally
Hammond **6** Eight (including division two of the national league)
7 True **8** Courtney Walsh **9** Robert **10** Matthew 'Steamy' Windows
11 David Lawrence **12** Yorkshire **13** Mark Alleyne **14** William Gilbert
15 Craig Spearman **16** Andrew Symonds **17** Jon Lewis
18 Charlie Parker **19** 1877 **20** 2000

Page 104

Hampshire CCC Answers

1 The Rose Bowl **2** Twice **3** Nottinghamshire **4** Jimmy Adams
5 True **6** Robin Smith **7** Mark Nicholas **8** Warwickshire **9** Cardigan
Connor **10** Justin Langer **11** Hawks **12** 1973 **13** Leicestershire
14 Derek Shackleton **15** Paul Jan Bakker **16** Neil Johnson **17** John
Crawley **18** Gordon Greenidge **19** Chris Tremlett **20** A crown and a
Tudor rose

Page 106

Kent CCC Answers

1 Kent Spitfires **2** The St Lawrence Ground **3** 1978 **4** The
Suffragettes **5** Geraint Jones **6** Allan Knott **7** Martin McCague
8 True **9** Pat Pocock **10** Derek Underwood **11** Amjad Khan
12 White **13** Frank Woolley **14** Gloucestershire **15** Mark Benson
16 David Fulton **17** Sanath Jayasuriya **18** Min Patel **19** Martin
Saggers **20** 2001

Page 108

Lancashire CCC Answers

1 Lancashire Lightning **2** True – he was born in Sheffield **3** 1934
4 Warren Hegg **5** Clive Lloyd **6** Arctic Monkeys **7** John Abrahams
8 Neil Fairbrother **9** Brian Statham **10** True **11** David Hughes
Page 110 **12** Glen Chapple **13** Joe Scuderi **14** Kyle Hogg **15** Andrew Flintoff
16 Phil Neville **17** Mike Atherton **18** Sajid Mahmood **19** Johnny
Briggs **20** Ernest Tyldesley

Leicestershire CCC Answers

1 Grace Road **2** 1998 **3** Yorkshire **4** Paul Nixon **5** Surrey
6 Leicestershire Foxes **7** Phil Simmons **8** Gary Lineker **9** Stuart
Broad and Jeremy Snape **10** David Gower **11** Alan Mullally **12** Essex
Page 112 **13** Gladstone Small – he's the only one not to play for Leicestershire
14 Oakham School **15** Raymond Illingworth **16** Les Taylor
17 James Whitaker **18** Chris Balderstone **19** South Africa **20** 1970s

Middlesex CCC Answers

1 The Crusaders **2** Baseball (and cricket) **3** Somerset **4** Ed Joyce and
Eoin Morgan **5** Henri **6** Owais Shah **7** Jason Gillespie **8** Mike Gatting
9 Pink – to raise awareness about breast cancer **10** Roland Butcher
Page 114 **11** Arsenal **12** Paul Downton **13** Psychotherapist **14** Seaxes
15 Warwickshire **16** John Emburey **17** Kent **18** Patsy Hendren
19 Fred Titmus **20** Wayne Daniel

Northamptonshire CCC Answers

1 Wantage Road **2** Never **3** Allan Lamb **4** Northamptonshire
Steelbacks **5** David Steele **6** David Capel and Rob Bailey
7 Leicestershire **8** India **9** Niall O'Brien **10** Mike Hussey **11** A Tudor
Page 116 rose **12** Wayne Larkins **13** Australia and South Africa **14** David Sales
15 Lancashire **16** Curtly Ambrose **17** Jason Brown **18** Lancashire
19 Dennis Brookes **20** Essex

Nottinghamshire CCC Answers

1 Stephen Fleming **2** The Outlaws **3** Franklyn Stephenson
4 Harold Larwood **5** Northamptonshire **6** Bruce French **7** Essex
8 Chris Broad and Tim Robinson **9** Clive Rice **10** Charlie Shreck
Page 118 **11** Derek Randall **12** Leicestershire **13** 2005 **14** Sir Richard Hadlee
15 Six feet 10 inches **16** Essex **17** George Gunn **18** Once
19 Dion Nash **20** Sir Garfield Sobers

Somerset CCC Answers

1 Viv Richards **2** Justin Langer **3** Sabres **4** Never **5** Lancashire
6 1974 **7** True **8** Joel Garner, Sunil Gavaskar and Brian Rose
9 Plasterer and tiler **10** True **11** Roland Lefebvre **12** Marcus
Page 120 Trescothick **13** Cameron White **14** Vic Marks **15** Allan Border
16 Arul Suppiah **17** Leicestershire **18** A dragon **19** Brian Close
20 Ian Blackwell

Surrey CCC Answers

1 The Brown Caps **2** Alistair Brown **3** True **4** Mark Butcher
5 Alec Stewart with 133 **6** Jack Hobbs **7** An amazing 496 for four
8 Warwickshire Bears **9** Jack Richards **10** Seven **11** Adam Hollioake
Page 122 **12** Martin Bicknell **13** Sir Alec Bedser **14** Sylvester Clarke **15** 1982
16 Middlesex **17** Lancashire **18** American Football **19** John Major
20 Julius Caesar

Sussex CCC Answers

1 Sharks **2** 2003 **3** Lancashire **4** Murray Goodwin with 335 not out
5 The Martlet **6** C. B. Fry **7** Ted Dexter **8** Leicestershire **9** False –
he was born in Germany **10** Mushtaq Ahmed **11** 1982 **12** Mark
Page 124 Robinson **13** Tony Greig **14** John Snow **15** West Indies **16** James
Kirtley **17** Mushtaq Ahmed, Saqlain Mushtaq and Rana Naved ul
Hasan **18** Lancashire **19** Warwickshire **20** Chris Adams

Warwickshire CCC Answers

1 Edgbaston **2** 1994 **3** The Natwest Trophy **4** Dennis Amiss
5 Eric Hollies **6** Asif Din **7** Dermot Reeve **8** Hampshire **9** Tom
Cartwright **10** Rohan Kanhai **11** The Bears **12** Geoff Humpage with
Page 126 13 **13** Gladstone Small **14** Middlesex **15** True **16** Tim Munton
17 Australia **18** Dougie Brown **19** Nick Knight **20** M. J. K. Smith

Worcestershire CCC Answers

1 Graeme Hick **2** Richard Illingworth **3** Neal Radford **4** Vikram
Solanki **5** Lancashire **6** Scunthorpe United and Lincoln City **7** Glen
Turner **8** 1988 and 1989 **9** Kabir Ali **10** 11 **11** True **12** Pear
Page 128 **13** Tom Moody **14** Tim Curtis **15** Warwickshire **16** Richard Hadlee
17 Vanburn Holder **18** Stuart Lampitt **19** Don Kenyon **20** Three

Yorkshire CCC Answers

1 Phoenix **2** Darren Gough **3** David Byas **4** Michael Parkinson
5 Sachin Tendulkar **6** Herbert Sutcliffe **7** True – he was born in
Manchester **8** Younis Khan **9** Damien Fleming **10** Somerset
Page 130 **11** 1983 **12** Len Hutton and Michael Vaughan **13** Ismail Dawood
14 Gerard Brophy **15** True **16** Adil Rashid **17** Fred Trueman
18 Wilfred Rhodes **19** False – he played for Manchester United
20 Martyn Moxon

Anagrams Answers

1 Brett Lee **2** Monty Panesar **3** Kevin Pietersen **4** Shane Warne
5 Muttiah Muralitharan **6** Ricky Ponting **7** Paul Collingwood
8 Sachin Tendulkar **9** Richard Hadlee **10** Ian Botham **11** Kapil Dev
Page 132 **12** Zaheer Khan **13** Sourav Ganguly **14** Curtly Ambrose **15** Michael
Vaughan **16** Daniel Vettori **17** Adam Gilchrist **18** Shaun Pollock
19 Mark Ramprakash **20** Younis Khan

Bad Boys Answers
1 Paul Collingwood **2** Dennis Lillee and Rodney Marsh **3** Ian Botham
4 Mohammed Azharuddin **5** Michael Atherton **6** Kiran More **7** Keith
Piper **8** Michael Holding **9** True **10** Jelly beans **11** Hansie Cronje
12 Mike Gatting **13** Rahul Dravid **14** Runako Morton **15** Wayne
Larkins **16** Andrew Symonds **17** Paul Smith **18** Terry Jenner
19 Chris Broad **20** David Gower and John Morris

Page 134

Beards and Moustaches Answers
1 Monty Panesar **2** Andrew Symonds and Muttiah Muralitharan
3 Mike Brearley **4** Shaun Udal **5** Richard Ellison **6** Phil DeFreitas
7 Andrew Flintoff **8** Mushtaq Ahmed **9** Merv Hughes **10** Hashim
Amla **11** Gloucestershire **12** David Boon **13** Mike Hendrick
14 Clive Lloyd **15** Saeed Anwar **16** Jack Russell **17** Allan Lamb and
Bruce Reid **18** Greg Chappell **19** Ewen Chatfield **20** Wayne Larkins

Page 136

Debuts Answers
1 Andrew Strauss **2** Shane Warne **3** 16 years and 205 days
4 Lawrence Rowe **5** 0 **6** Narendra Hirwani **7** Dominic Cork
8 Mohammad Ashraful **9** Sachin Tendulkar **10** Gavin Hamilton
11 Australia **12** Brian Close **13** They all made a duck on their Test
debut **14** Geoff Greenidge **15** Mohammad Azharuddin **16** England
17 Damien Fleming **18** Lee Germon **19** Brendon Kuruppu
20 Jacques Rudolph

Page 138

Family Affairs Answers
1 Adam and Ben Hollioake **2** False – he's the son of bowler Peter
Pollock **3** Steve and Mark Waugh **4** Gary and Mark Butcher, Adam and
Ben Hollioake and Martin and Darren Bicknell **5** Nick Price **6** Arnie
Sidebottom **7** Russell Crowe **8** Niall and Kevin O'Brien **9** Ed Joyce for
England and Dominick Joyce for Ireland **10** Chris Broad and his son
Stuart Broad **11** The Headleys. George and his son Ron played for West
Indies. Ron's son Dean played for England **12** Pedro Collins **13** John
Benaud **14** Greg Chappell instructed brother Trevor Chappell **15**
Simon Jones (his father is Jeff Jones) **16** Tony and Ian Greig **17** Carl
Greenidge (his father is Gordon Greenidge) **18** Denis Compton's
grandson Nick and Len Hutton's grandson Ben played for Middlesex
19 Roy and Ken Palmer **20** Alec and Micky Stewart

Page 140

Golden Grahams Answers
1 Graeme Hick **2** Graham Gooch **3** Durham **4** Graham Rose
5 New Zealand **6** Graeme Wood **7** Debyshire **8** Graeme Swann
9 Graeme Fowler **10** Graeme Smith **11** Graham Dilley **12** Surrey
13 False – he's the son of David Lloyd **14** Graham Yallop **15** Graham
Cowdrey **16** Graham Stevenson **17** Graham Wagg **18** Australia
19 41 **20** Graeme Labrooy

Page 142

Injuries Answers

1 A cricket ball **2** Steve Waugh **3** Nasser Hussain **4** Terry Alderman
5 Malcolm Marshall **6** Ted Dexter **7** Ian Greig **8** Motorised luggage
trolley **9** Malcolm Marshall **10** David Lawrence **11** Mike Gatting
Page 144 **12** Chris Lewis **13** The Gabba in Brisbane **14** Andrew Strauss
15 Rick McCosker **16** Anil Kumble **17** Ezra Moseley **18** Derek
Pringle **19** Will Jefferson **20** True

Name Game Answers

1 Pigeon **2** Viv Richards **3** Gordon Greenidge **4** Ashley Giles
5 Stuart Clark **6** Steve Waugh **7** Geoff Lawson **8** Robbie Williams
9 Rugby league **10** Vic Marks **11** Ricky Ponting **12** The Invincibles
Page 146 **13** Chris Adams **14** Gladstone Small **15** Chaminda Vaas **16** The
Gaffer **17** *Thunderbirds* **18** Bob Dylan **19** Hubert **20** Nixon McLean

One Test Wonders Answers

1 Alan Jones **2** Joey Benjamin **3** Mark Benson **4** Gavin Hamilton
5 Stuart Law **6** Gareth Breese **7** South Africa **8** Andy Lloyd
9 Mick Malone **10** Matt Nicholson **11** Paul Parker **12** Mike Smith
Page 148 **13** Simon Brown **14** West Indies **15** Neil Williams **16** Andy
Ganteaume **17** Rodney Redmond **18** Alan Butcher **19** Tony Pigott
20 Ryan Sidebottom and his father Arnie

Portly Players Answers

1 Botham and Eddie (Hemmings) **2** Mike Gatting **3** Ian Austin
4 Andy Moles **5** Ramesh Powar **6** David Sales **7** Andrew Flintoff
8 Rob Key **9** Inzamam-ul-Haq **10** Shane Warne **11** Colin Milburn
Page 150 **12** Mark Taylor **13** Jack Simmons **14** David Boon **15** Arjuna
Ranatunga **16** Jimmy Ormond **17** William 'Fatty' Foulke **18** Mark
Cosgrove **19** Greg Ritchie **20** The Big Ship

Quotes Answers

1 Nathan Astle who now has over 50 Test wickets **2** Ashley Giles after
dropping Ricky Ponting at Adelaide in 2006 **3** Martin McGuinness
4 Alastair Cook **5** Ryan Sidebottom **6** Robin Williams **7** Harold Pinter
Page 152 **8** Bishan Bedi **9** Tony Greig **10** Geoffrey Boycott **11** Owais Shah
12 The 2007 FA Cup Final **13** Billy Bowden **14** Andrew Flintoff
15 Andrew Flintoff again **16** Mike Gatting **17** Terry Alderman
18 Jeff Thomson **19** Dietmar Hamman **20** Vikram Solanki

All Rounders Answers

1 Ian Botham **2** Garry Sobers and Jacques Kallis **3** Imran Khan and
Ian Botham **4** Kapil Dev **5** Worcestershire and Sussex **6** Shane
Watson **7** Ronni Irani **8** Chris Cairns **9** Paul Collingwood **10** Richie
Page 154 Benaud **11** Carl Hooper **12** Ian Botham **13** Jeff Wilson **14** Rikki
Clarke **15** Denis Compton **16** Tony Greig **17** Waqar Younis
18 Peter and Shaun Pollock and Lance and Chris Cairns **19** Shaun
Pollock **20** Andy Goram

Big Hitters Answers

1 Garry Sobers, Ravi Shastri, Herschelle Gibbs and Yuvraj Singh **2** Andrew Symonds **3** Dimitri Mascarenhas **4** Viv Richards **5** Chris Gayle **6** Shahid Afridi **7** Kevin Pietersen **8** 57 **9** Mohammad Ashraful **10** Ian Botham **11** Harbhajan Singh **12** Chris Cairns **13** Andrew Flintoff **14** Wasim Akram **15** Ali Brown **16** Sanath Jayasuriya **17** 194 **18** Cameron White **19** Chris Gayle **20** Arthur Wellard

Page 156

Captains Answers

1 Steve Waugh **2** Stephen Fleming **3** Paul Colingwood **4** 1988 **5** Mike Gatting, John Emburey, Chris Cowdrey and Graham Gooch **6** Graeme Smith **7** Mark Butcher **8** Allan Lamb **9** Michael Atherton **10** Waqar Younis **11** Garry Sobers **12** Two **13** Allan Border **14** They all made a pair on their debut as captain **15** Kepler Wessels **16** Khaled Mashud of Bangladesh and Ian Botham **17** Clive Lloyd **18** Steve Waugh with 111 **19** Sourav Ganguly **20** Graham Gooch

Page 158

In The Field Answers

1 Andrew Strauss **2** Five **3** Ian Botham **4** Herschelle Gibbs **5** Kiran More **6** Viv Richards **7** Four by Younis Khan against Bangladesh in 2001 **8** Allan Border **9** Four **10** Shane Warne **11** Six **12** Jonty Rhodes **13** Roger Harper **14** Allan Donald and Lance Klusener **15** Ricky Ponting **16** Mohammad Azharuddin **17** Five **18** He hit the ball into Allan Lamb's boot and was caught by David Gower **19** Mark Taylor **20** Neil Harvey. His full name is Neil Harvey Fairbrother

Page 160

Left Arm Seamers Answers

1 Wasim Akram and Chaminda Vaas **2** Zaheer Khan **3** Nathan Bracken and Mitchell Johnson **4** Geoff Allott **5** Alan Mullally **6** Irfan Pathan **7** Wasim Akram **8** John Lever **9** Alan Davidson **10** Chaminda Vaas **11** New Zealand **12** Queensland **13** Paul Taylor **14** Irfan Pathan, Zaheer Khan, R. P. Singh, Murali Kartik and Yuvraj Singh **15** Yorkshire **16** Sohail Tanvir **17** West Indies **18** Mark Ilott **19** One **20** 104

Page 162

Left Arm Spinners Answers

1 Monty Panesar **2** Michael Clarke **3** 297 **4** Phil Simmons **5** New Zealand **6** Daniel Vettori **7** Brad Hogg **8** Bishan Bedi **9** Gary Keedy **10** Phil Edmonds **11** Tony Lock **12** Ravi Shastri **13** Alf Valentine **14** Wilfred Rhodes **15** Omar Henry **16** Warwickshire **17** Min Patel **18** Tendulkar **19** Paul Adams **20** Iqbal Qasim

Page 164

Left-Handed Batsmen Answers

1 David Gower **2** Kepler Wessels **3** South Africa **4** Graham Pollock **5** Graham Thorpe **6** Mark Taylor **7** Nick Knight **8** Graeme Smith **9** Somerset **10** True **11** Sourav Ganguly **12** Stephen Fleming **13** John Edrich **14** Larry Gomes **15** Shivnarine Chanderpaul **16** Andy Flower **17** Graham Thorpe **18** Mike Hussey **19** Darren Lehmann **20** Sanath Jayasuriya

Page 166

Off Spinners Answers

1 Jim Laker **2** Lance Gibbs **3** Gareth Batty **4** Saqlain Mushtaq
5 Peter Such **6** Nathan Hauritz **7** 36 **8** Greg Matthews **9** India
10 Tim May **11** Srinivasaraghavan Venkataraghavan **12** Raymond
Illingworth **13** Harbhajan Singh **14** New Zealand **15** John Traicos
16 Pat Symcox **17** John Emburey **18** Kamran Akmal and M. S. Dhoni
19 Vic Marks **20** Pat Pocock

Page 168

Opening Batsmen Answers

1 Andrew Strauss **2** Michael Atherton **3** Gordon Greenidge and
Desmond Haynes with 6,482 **4** 380 by Matthew Hayden **5** Sunil
Gavaskar **6** Sachin Tendulkar and Sourav Ganguly **7** Marcus
Trescothick and Vikram Solanki **8** Middlesex **9** South Africa **10** Ian
Botham **11** Rahul Dravid and Virender Sehwag **12** Graeme Smith
13 Graeme Fowler **14** Middlesex and Somerset **15** True **16** Alastair
Cook **17** Mudassar Nazar who took 557 minutes to reach three
figures **18** Michael Atherton **19** Jason Gallian **20** Australia

Page 170

Record Breakers - Test Matches Answers

1 Sri Lanka compiled the mammoth score against India in 1997
2 Brian Lara **3** West Indies chased down Australia **4** 26 **5** 16 **6** 21
7 West Indies **8** 588 **9** Six **10** Wasim Akram with 12 **11** Muttiah
Muralitharan **12** 90 **13** Kapil Dev with nine for 83 **14** Shane Warne
15 Jim Laker **16** Sonny Ramadhin **17** Kumar Sangakkara and Mahela
Jayawardene **18** Mark Waugh with 181 **19** Kiran More **20** 153

Page 172

Record Breakers - One Day Internationals Answers

1 257 runs **2** Sri Lanka against Holland in 2006 **3** 35 **4** 21 **5** West
Indies bowled 37 wides against Pakistan in 1989 **6** Sachin Tendulkar
7 Saeed Anwar with 194 **8** Dennis Amiss and Desmond Haynes
9 Zaheer Abbas, Saeed Anwar and Herschelle Gibbs **10** Wasim Akram
11 Shahid Afridi **12** 17 **13** Mick Lewis **14** Tendulkar and Dravid
15 Shoaib Akhtar with 43 **16** Dougie Brown **17** Phil Simmons took
four for three from 10 overs against Pakistan in 1992 **18** Darren
Gough **19** 438 **20** Two

Page 174

Smell The Leather - Pacemen Answers

1 Shoaib Akhtar **2** Nick Knight **3** Michael Atherton **4** England
5 West Indies **6** Frank Tyson **7** Shane Bond **8** Fidel Edwards
9 Fred Trueman **10** Allan Donald **11** Bob Willis **12** Malcolm
Marshall at 20.95 **13** Lasith Malinga **14** John Snow **15** 'You guys
are history' **16** He took nine for 57 **17** Graham Dilley **18** Waqar
Younis **19** Simon Jones **20** Patrick Patterson

Page 176

Swingers and Seamers Answers

1 Matthew Hoggard **2** Terry Alderman **3** Matthew Hoggard **4** Bob
Massie **5** Angus Fraser **6** Don Shepherd **7** Javagal Srinath **8** Michael
Atherton **9** Dean Headley **10** Darren Gough **11** Andrew Caddick
12 Makhaya Ntini **13** Andrew Hall **14** Ottis Gibson **15** West Indies
16 Merv Hughes **17** Steve Perryman **18** Heath Streak **19** Sarfraz
Nawaz **20** Alec Bedser

Page 178

Tail Enders Answers

Page 180

1 Rabbits **2** Courtney Walsh **3** Bob Holland **4** Bob Willis **5** Chris Martin **6** Mushtaq Ahmed **7** New Zealand **8** Devon Malcolm **9** Geoff Allott **10** Jason Gillespie **11** Steve Harmison with 42 **12** Brett Lee and Michael Kasprowicz **13** Alan Mullally **14** Danny Morrison **15** Phil Tufnell **16** Mark Robinson **17** 75 **18** Zaheer Khan **19** India **20** Courtney Walsh

West Indian Bowlers Answers

Page 182

1 Courtney Walsh **2** Michael Holding **3** Colin Croft **4** Lance Gibbs, Malcolm Marshall, Curtly Ambrose and Courtney Walsh **5** Jermaine Lawson **6** Winston and Kenneth Benjamin **7** Joel Garner **8** Wes Hall **9** Andy Roberts **10** Middlesex **11** Michael Holding **12** Malcolm Marshall 20.95 **13** Ian Bishop **14** Wes Hall **15** Patrick Patterson **16** Jack Noreiga took nine for 95 against India in 1970 **17** Franklyn Stephenson **18** Daren Powell **19** Curtly Ambrose and Courtney Walsh **20** Surrey

Wicketkeepers Answers

Page 184

1 Alan Knott with 95 **2** 82 **3** Ian Healy **4** Rodney Marsh **5** Matt Prior **6** Seven **7** Dennis Lillee and Rodney Marsh **8** Andy Flower with 232 **9** 173 by Alec Stewart **10** Kiran More with five **11** Jeff Dujon **12** Papua New Guinea **13** Mark Boucher and Ian Healy with 67 **14** Dwayne Bravo **15** Six **16** Jack Russell **17** Syed Kirmani **18** Wasim Bari with 228 **19** Ian Gould **20** Vikram Solanki

Wrist Spinners Answers

Page 186

1 Shane Warne **2** Chris Schofield **3** Abdul Qadir **4** Laxman Sivaramakrishnan **5** Collins Obuya **6** Stuart Macgill **7** Trevor Hohns **8** Mushtaq Ahmed **9** True **10** Rawl Lewis **11** Clarrie Grimmett **12** Ian Salisbury **13** Anil Kumble **14** Essex **15** Adil Rashid **16** Piyush Chawla **17** Paul Strang **18** Wasim Akram and Dilip Vengsarkar **19** Bernard Bosanquet **20** Terry Jenner

Books Answers

Page 188

1 Ted Dexter **2** Richard Blakey **3** Simon Hughes **4** Ian Botham **5** Phil Tufnell **6** Duncan Fletcher **7** 1864 **8** Steve James **9** Steve Waugh **10** Paul Smith **11** Passion **12** Tom Cartwright **13** Clive Lloyd **14** Fire **15** Jack Iverson **16** Jonathan Agnew **17** Shane Warne **18** Mike Brearley **19** David Lloyd **20** Dickie Bird

Grounds Answers

Page 190

1 The Melbourne Cricket Ground **2** Leicestershire **3** Trent Bridge **4** India **5** Zimbabwe **6** The MCG **7** Cape Town **8** New Zealand **9** The St Lawrence Ground in Canterbury, Kent **10** The Pavilion End and The Nursery End **11** The Fremantle Doctor **12** The Oval **13** Sheffield United's Bramall Lane hosted one Test match in 1902 **14** Jamaica **15** The Antigua Recreation Ground **16** Pakistan **17** Glamorgan **18** Surrey **19** Mumbai **20** Headingley